VERNON

A VISITOR'

DRAMA

OR

OEDIPUS WHO ?

A VERY FRACTURED REVIEW

ALL YOU MAY NEED TO KNOW ABOUT IT
AND NO MORE

VERNON VAS ELLIOTT

A VISITOR'S GUIDE TO

GREEK DRAMA

OR

OEDIPUS WHO?

AN EFFORTLESS, SPICY, BAWDY, IRREVERENT, SACRELIGIOUS, DISRESPECTFUL TOUR THROUGH ANCIENT SOAP OPERAS

FREE

PRONUNCIATION GUIDE

OF THE UNPRONOUNCABLE

EFSTATHIADIS GROUP S.A.
14, Valtetsiou Str.
106 80 Athens
Tel: (01) 5154650, 6450113
Fax: (01) 5154657
GREECE

ISBN 960 226 491 8

Printed and bound in Greece

To all of us who have been frustrated by Academia, Academics, Academicians and have been bored ad infinitum, but lived to tell about it.

WHY?
A pretence at a prologue

Very often I find myself laughing at tragedy and crying over comedy. I have not as yet been able to figure out this contradiction or incongruity. It is perhaps that I do not quite understand human dilemmas or that I have a distorted if not perverted sense of the tragic. I am not sure which is true. As a matter of fact, the older I grow the less sure I am of anything let alone comedy and tragedy. So, I tried to understand a bit about those things and I came upon a rather ..... tragic and ominous wall: ACADEMIA. Oh my dear Gods! Could it be that they (the academicians I mean, not the Gods) made the tragic comic and the comic tragic? I would not be surprised at all. So I took the alternative that seemed a lot more attractive. I went to fly my kites and ponder my next step. Lo and behold, holding onto those strings against the indomitable winds of Sounion, I had a brilliant idea, which is quite an accomplishment for a far less than brilliant mind! WRITE A BOOK!! Why not? I knew damn little about the subject, I admit. It would force me to discover things and present them in a palatable, digested way to you my dear reader. ECCO!!! And here it is. This is the Why. The How, I will not bore you with at length. I just went to the library - in the US because there is more on the subject there than in Greece - got a whole bunch of books, and I started reading and keeping notes. That was some twenty years ago. My library fines must be higher than my income taxes. Seriously though, I just came across my notes when cleaning out old moving boxes. I updated my info and my notes - not much has changed since then - and put this little thing together for you. Hope you enjoy it.

V.V.E.

CONTENTS

I

BACKGROUND

You may ask "Is this necessary? I just want the facts. Give me the story line, the plot, don't want no background." Well, there are a few would-be eggheads, wanna-be eggheads, and pseudo-eggheads, like me that have a need to know - and soon forget - backgrounds. A little background never hurt anyone, I always say, and it costs so little, just 20 drachmas a kilo. Next to nothing.

HELLAS - Greece to the Greeks. A peninsula roughly 45,000 square miles, almost the size of Maine, in the southeastern part of Europe. Hellas - with a very very silent H - is covered 80% by mountains, the highest of which is Mount Olympus in Thessaly - Central Greece. Altitude 10,000 feet.

IMPORTANT REGIONS

1	MACEDONIA	Northern Greece
2	THESSALIA	South of Macedonia
3	PHOKIS	Central - Delphi
4	BEOTIA	SE of Phokis - Thebes
5	ATTICA	SE of Beotia - Athens
6	PELOPONNESUS	Southern Greece

Shaped like a maple leaf.Sparta.Corinth. Mycenae

7	THE CYCLADES	Numerous islands Mid-Aegean Sea
8	CRETE	Large island South Aegean.Knossos

9 ASIA MINOR - ANATOLIA

A EOLIS

B IONIA

C DORIS

D HELLESPONT

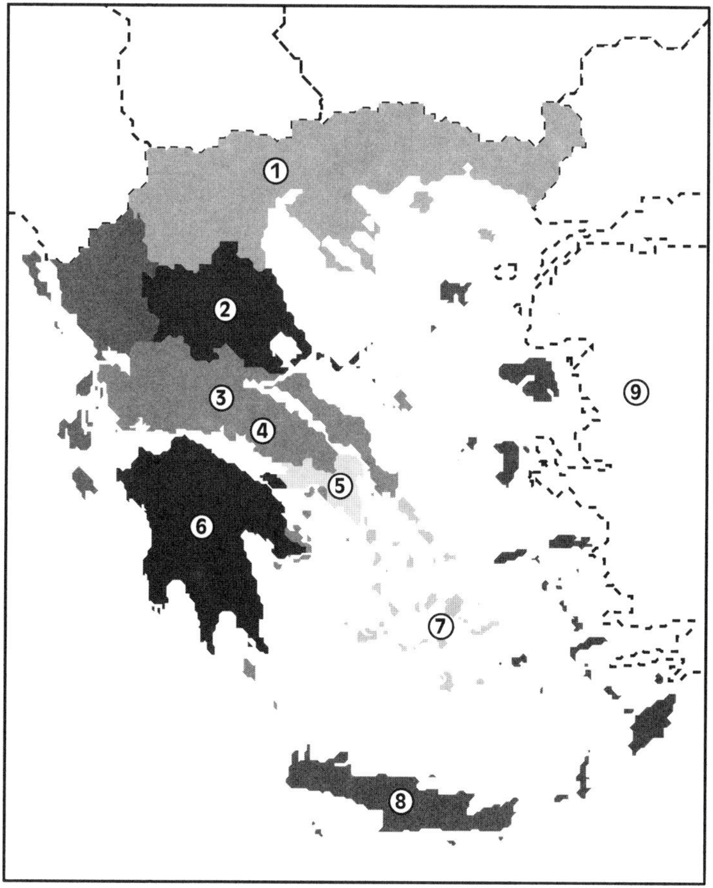
1
2
3
4
5
6
7
8
9

The geography of the region was very important in its cultural- political development. Now isn't this quite a statement? What it actually means is that communication was difficult back in those days. It still is as a matter of fact, but for entirely different reasons. So, instead of one nation we had a bunch of city states that spoke roughly the same language but did not communicate too well and were constantly feuding and fighting one another, except when they were invaded by strangers that spoke a different language, like the Persians, the Incas and the Polyesters. Historians say that Crete was the first part of Europe to be civilized. I wonder what has happened since then.

The sea is called the Aegean Sea and to the west of the peninsula the Ionian Sea. For the sake of brevity we'll lump it all together and call it the Aegean Civilization because that is what historians call it.

In the beginning, 3000 BC, give or take a few hours, there were some natives that lived there peacefully, fishing and hunting and frolicking and generally having the time of their prehistoric lives. In Crete, there were the Minoans and in Peloponnesus the Myceneans. The Minoans were a quiet crowd and minded their own business, building palaces for their king Minos and worshipping ..... the Bull. And why not? Did you expect them to know any better way back in say 1843 BC? Now I'm not making this up. Just check with any Greek.

The Myceneans lived in Peloponnesus and were much more prone to invasions. Marauding and pillaging invaders from the north came soon enough. You see it was too cold up there and some of them got together and said "Hey, this is no way to live, you can't even get out in the winter time and have a decent capuccino somewhere." So pretty much like today's Florida is invaded by Canadians, Iowans and assorted other northerners, the Dorians (1100 BC) the Aeolians and the Ionians decided to move south and get warm. They did so from somewhere in the bowels of frozen northern Europe. It was a destructive and violent invasion, similar to what happened to Florida. I mean just go down US 1 and imagine the place without all those gaudy neon signs. What a wonderful beach it must have been at one time.

Well, the invaders assimilated the locals properly and settled down to "civilize" the area. The Dorians brought with them iron,- see, they didn't come empty handed. With iron and some letters they stole from the Phoenicians to the south, and plenty of time, sitting in their beach chairs enjoying the sun and the local fruits and the wine, they had nothing else to do but dream up wild ideas like adding vowels to the alphabet and writing stories for their amusement. Just about anyone can see what a great improvement adding vowels can be. The language became more flexible and melodious. How can anyone pronounce, let alone write poetry with words like

STRNGTH, or WTSPKR and FCC. These folks also created a huge vocabulary for their day. Surely they did not have clever phrases like "user friendly" or "remote control" or even "telephone", but they did have ones such as Oedipus complex, Deus-ex-machina, history, philosophy, psychology etc. which adorn the Latin as well as the anglo-saxon dictionaries today.

Gradually the migratory wars settled down after a few hundred years and slowly, with a lot of spare time on their hands, a good language, iron and a few slaves to do the labor, they started ..... thinking. And good thinkers they were. We still use their thoughts today. They called themselves Hellenes collectively. The word Greeks, came along a lot later. By the time we come to 500 BC these guys were quite well organized into city states. We call them city states because they were not one country as we recognize a country today. The Dorians who settled in Sparta were conservative and busied themselves with the martial arts and defense since the helots (slaves) were doing the real work. From morning to night and from birth to death, they were dedicated to the state.

The Ionians settled around Athens. As a hobby they decided to create Government, which of course led to politics. Well, you know how power corrupts. After a variety of trial and error games, a few lynchings, assassinations and the like, a man by the strange name of

Cleisthenes (Clee-sthe`-nis) in 508 BC at 10.00 am came up with the idea of Democracy. It, Democracy I mean, was supposed to be a way of governing that gave the illusion that all the citizens were empowered and they could all vote regardless of wealth and tribal association. What goes on behind the scenes is anything but Democracy - but at least it gives the impression of being fair and free. Today 2500 years later, I am willing to bet that there are quite a few modern Greeks that don't think it was such a bright idea that Cleisthenes had in the first place. But we are stuck with it for the time being. If you'd like to read more about modern Greece and the results of 2500 years of "democracy", look for my other books mentioned on a page somewhere near the end of this book.

Some of the Athenians in those days were not amused by the goings-on, however. One of them AESCHYLUS (pronounced E`s-hee-lus) thought one morning "Enough of this politics thing already. I am going to write and produce and direct a few plays for the amusement of my fellow Athenians." Nobody had ever heard of such a thing before. In that respect Athens was something like what Hollywood, CA is today where no one has ever heard of a play either.

Here I am going to insert a giant footnote, perhaps the largest one in history and give you some semi-academic background on the origins of tragedy as this is what

Aeschylus wrote. It won't be too painful or ..... tragic. I promise. Besides, I will throw in a few illustrations, home made by the way.

Have you ever wondered why actor groups are called "thespians"? Well it is because the father of drama was Thespis. Now it all makes good sense, you see. And if you think I am making this up, check with your encyclopaedia and if you don't have one, it's high time you bought a set.

Well, Thespis is the one who created the very first school of actors or hypocrites as he liked to call them. I bet you Sylvester Stalone doesn't know that one! And you do!

The actor performed at intermissions of the Dithyramb (dee-thee-ram) which was a choral, lyric, religious ceremony performed in honor of Dionysus, the God of wine and frolicking and fun of all sorts. The men in the chorus, for some strange reason, were dressed in goat skins. Who knows it may have been the polyester of the day. A male goat is called TRAGOS. ODIA means song so we have a goat-song or TRAGODIA or TRAGEDY. See how easy background really is?

Seriously, the men in the chorus represented Satyrs, companions of Dionysus who, according to Greek mythology, were half goat and half men. Now, how much of this you want to believe is up to you. The leader of the chorus would improvise the story. So Thespis created the first real actor and the beginning of tragedy had its roots in a religious ceremony.

Eventually, new myths were created. You see we humans need myths and it was inevitable that new events would create new myths and even new gods. And the chorus no longer wore goat skins but attire appropriate to the story. In "Gidget goes to Hawaii" for example we see that this custom still holds and all the chorus wears bikinis.

Aeschylus added a secular actor and a third actor was added by Sophocles later on. Much much later on, Americans elected, in jest it must have been, an actor as a president, thus having fun with both actors and democracy. This is what we call today our Greek legacy.

But I digress. The chorus was fixed at 15, its part gradually diminishing in favor of dialogue between the actors. Dialogue came to its climax in the movie "Marty" with the unforgettable Ernest Borgnine and his friend spending the major part of the movie asking each other: "What do you wanna do tonite Marty?" "Dunno, what do you wanna do?" "Dunno, whata ya wanna do?" and so on.

The plays were short and came in bunches of four, something like what we call skits today. For those of you that want to get really technical they are called

TETRALOGIES. TETRA being the prefix for four as you well know. The first three, the TRILOGY, were at first on one theme but later on to provide more variety they were based on different themes. Whoever thought that marketing is a modern science? The fourth skit was a SATYR play somewhat lighter in nature and having something to do with Dionysus, lest he get mad and do away with all fun and games for the humans.

The CHORUS had a number of tasks. To begin with, it was a means of expression both in poetry and motion. It also interpreted events. You know, sometimes you see a movie today and you come out not knowing what the whole thing was about. Well, this did not happen in ancient times because the chorus was there. The chorus also relieved tension, talked to the actors, giving them advice when they felt like it,and also information about preceding events, sort of a forerunner of today's Flashback.

The plays were produced by the state for a celebration called DIONYSIA, in honor of you-know-who, in early spring each year.There were prizes handed out too, something like today's OSCARS. The prizes went to the best poet,the best leading actor- the protagonist- and the sponsor -horegos. The more things change the more they remain the same! The jury was selected by lot . This was real democracy at work. By the way, there were no actresses in those days. The actors played both male and female roles and several of them not just one. They wore masks and wigs and a special shoe called COTHURNUS with a high sole which gave added dignity to the actor. Now there's an enterprising idea for anyone who perchance is business minded. Open a COTHORNUS-MART in Hollywood!! and call it C-MART or get into a COTHURNUS FACTORY. Madonna would probably be a great customer. By the way, admission was either free or at a nominal fee.

So drama was almost like a Wagnerian opera, a poetic musical tragedy, with mythological subjects and religious and ethical instruction as a theme. Each play was short, somewhere between 900 and 1700 lines. Unlike today's TV, there was no violent action, no horror scenes. They were reported to the audience sometimes by a messenger. Now these were people of real taste!! Interestingly there were no subplots and there was no location change. It all took place in one location beginning to end and no lapses in time. At most, it all took place in one day. Today we have acts and scenes. Well back then the first act was the PROLOGUE, then came PARODOS - the entrance of others and directly after it EPISODES. Action after the episodes were the STASIMA choral odes and finally EXODOS - action after the last ode.

One last thing. APO MIHANIS THEOS in Greek better-known by its Latin-adopted title DEUS EX-MACHINA was a crane-like technical device on top of the scene from which a dummy was suspended - a real one, not a person - representing a God and it gave sort of a miraculous end to the play. Euripides used it a lot. His plots contained so many dilemmas where only a God could solve them. I kind of wish Marty had had a DEUS EX-MACHINA.

Now wasn't this a long footnote? But full of juicy information, wouldn't you say? And worth every drachma?

How could I possibly forget to say something about the theatron itself? I guess this is as good a spot as any.

THEATRON was the part of the theater where the people sat. They say that a picture is worth 1000 V.V.Elliott pages so here is a very modest sketch of the whole ODION.

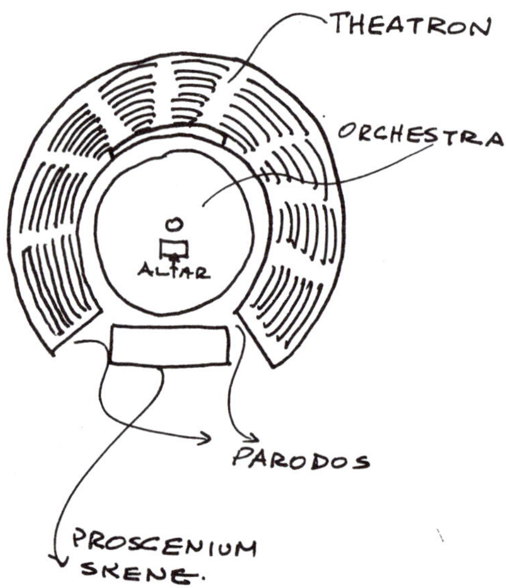

THEATRON was actually the part of the ODION for the audience. Conveniently carved out of a hillside and as circular as possible, its ......bleachers were made of marble or local stone.Front row seats were available of course for priests of Dionysus and other VIPs.The seating capacity of the theater of Dionysus in Athens was 17000 give or take a few Athenians

ORCHESTRA was the middle circular section where the chorus dragged their feet, the actors acted -mostly in front of the proscenium-and the priests performed sacrifices for everyone's delight as an opening act more or less.

PROSCENIUM was the facade of the building that usually had three doorways and was the palace or temple where the play took place.The back of the Proscenium was the SKENE which was no more than a dressing room for the actors. To the right and left of the prosceniun-skene was PARODOS , the entrance and exit of the chorus. No curtains anywhere in sight.

Enough said already. Let's go on to the next chapter.

II

TRAGEDY

A - AESCHYLUS

Back to **AESCHYLUS.** (Es-hee-lus)

I will not say much about the man (I am planning another book on biographies) other than to say that he was also a soldier who fought at the battles of Salamis and Marathon. Born 525 BC, he died at 70 years of age in Sicily 455 BC. He wrote about 90 plays in his career and was the real innovator of drama as he added a second actor and reduced the importance of the chorus.

His existing plays are:

1. The Suppliants
2. The Persians
3. Seven against Thebes
4. Prometheus Bound
5. Agamemnon
6. Choephoroi (Libation Bearers) HOY-FO'RY
7. Eumenides

The last three - a trilogy - are also called together the ORESTEIA.

AESCHYLUS wrote trilogies on a single theme. His plots were uncomplicated with little action. There is little or no development in his characters. They suffer not because of character faults but rather because of sin, marching to their inevitable gloom or doom or both.

Aeschylus was a religious thinker that dealt with profound moral and religious problems pretty much like say Jerry

Falwell or Oral Roberts today only better. He purified primitive religion based on vengeance (Stalone - Swartzeneger - Van Damm-Bruce Lee - Eastwood) to an ethical monotheism (belief in one God) the ultimate goodness. But he did say that you pay for your sins and excessive pride is one of them. Wisdom comes after suffering and because of our human limitations we must subordinate ourselves to the wisdom of the state and the Gods.

I do have my doubts about his reasoning because today I know of no state with wisdom in its authority. As for the Gods, that's a bit too touchy a subject for this book. Perhaps in another one.

In this "light" version for the sake of brevity we will deal only in Prometheus Bound and the Oresteia. Now if enough books are sold maybe I'll do a Volume II with the rest.

PROMETHEUS BOUND

Here we must again digress momentarily for some mythological background without which the story may be meaningless.

Rulers of the universe were the TITANS and their King CRONUS (Saturn in Latin). He had six children, who eventually through social climbing became Olympian Gods. ZEUS, the leader of the Gods, revolted against CRONUS and overthrew him. So what's new you might ask.

Oceanus and Prometheus deserted the TITANS and sided with Zeus. The TITANS were defeated as Zeus and Prometheus used intelligence - something like the CIA - rather than brute force. The TITANS were exiled somewhere, I don't remember where, and their King CRONUS elsewhere lest they conspire again, and ATLAS, poor Atlas, because of his brutal strength was left holding the earth on his shoulders. (Now you know how that came about.)

Zeus sat on his throne prettily and started giving orders as the new ruler of the Universe. He said to Prometheus: "Hey Prom." He called him Prom for short. "Prom, how about making an imperfect creature we can have some fun with?" And Prometheus created the Greeks and appointed himself their benefactor and protector. But men grew evil and Zeus started to get uncomfortable with the whole idea because of this war and that war and conflicts and dilemmas and problems, problems, problems all the time. They gave him a headache. Not only that, but he had Hera to contend with, his wife, and his girlfriend, Io (pronounced EE-O') at the time, giving him problems galore. So he decided to destroy the Greeks and rid himself of that problem at least. Good old Prometheus though, defended the Greeks and defied Zeus' edict. He stole fire which Zeus had forbidden and gave it to the Greeks to better their life and defend themselves. Zeus got furious and started swearing and cussing, calling Prom all sorts of unprintable epithets. Had we taped that outburst it would have been full of bleeps - something almost as bad as the Nixon tapes.

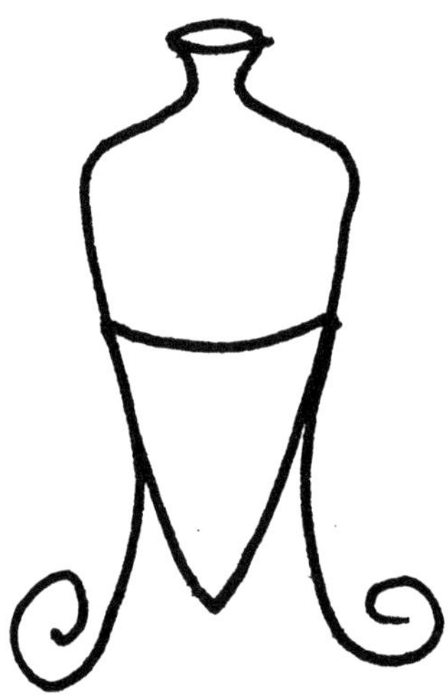

CHARACTERS

Power and Force	servants of Zeus
Hephestus	ironsmith of the Gods (a lesser God himself)
Prometheus	Titan
Oceanus	Titan
Io (EE-O)	Zeus' lover at the time
Hermes	postmaster general for Zeus
Chorus	daughters of Oceanus

PLOT

PROLOGUE (lines 1 - 127)

Power and Force bring in Prometheus, dragging him on the ground. Zeus, who hadn't had a good day thus far, orders Hephestus to bind Prom to a rock in a desolate gloomy area called Scythia to punish him for giving fire to man. Heph doesn't want to because he likes Prom. Besides, they are relatives and friends. But he is afraid of Zeus. Reluctantly, Heph under the ruthless directives of Power shackles Prom on the rock who remains silent and dignified until he is left alone when defiantly but with much pain he bemoans his fate.

PARODOS (lines 128 - 192)

The Oceanids, lovely innocent and sweet, enter as the Chorus and express their compassion toward poor Prom and disapproval of Zeus' capricious and arbitrary behaviour. Prom, always a gentleman, tries to comfort them instead and hints that he's got one over Zeus, and he is going to tell all, unless Zeus removes his bonds. What Prom knows is that if Zeus, who's been after Thetis for some time, gets Thetis, they'll have a son who will overthrow him. Something like The Bold and the Beautiful in other words.

FIRST EPISODE (lines 193 - 396)

The Chorus is curious as to what had transpired. Prom tells them the whole thing from the beginning. He tells them how he had helped Zeus against the Titans, how Zeus got his nose up in the air after that, and that Zeus punished him for saving man and giving him fire. 'Oceanus enters on a Pegasus which was a winged horse extinct today since the invention of the airplane. He too expresses sympathy and friendship toward Prom and advises him to give in to Zeus for his own good and he offers to mediate the situation for him. Prom though cautions Oceanus that he himself may be in danger. Oceanus feels useless, loses his temper and exits.

FIRST STASIMON (lines 397 - 435)

The Chorus mourns the suffering of Prometheus and Atlas.

SECOND EPISODE (lines 436-525)

Prom recalls the benefits of mankind, who now with fire in their hands can smoke cigarettes and create a whole bunch of new inventions that we call "civilization" things like chateaubriant and chicken cordon bleu. He states that Fate has predicted that he will be released and hints at the secret he knows about Zeus.

SECOND STASIMON (lines 526 - 560)

The Chorus feels sorry for Prometheus and pities him but it expresses awe and reverence for Zeus and tells Prom how imperfect and limited man is and advises moderation.

THIRD EPISODE (lines 561 - 886)

Io, transformed into a cow - Zeus did that frequently with ex-lovers - is pursued by an insect which is none other than the ghost of Argus. She rants and raves about how much she has suffered because of Zeus and after hearing Prom's story reveals to him her own deep secret, how Zeus had gotten to her and her father found out and drove her out of the house in disgust, how Zeus had turned her into a heifer or was it a geurnsey I don't remember, how Hera jealous sent Argus who had 100 eyes to pursue her, how Hermes killed Argus but a stinging fly urged on by Argus' ghost was making her life miserable. Prom then, being a prophet as well, tells her that she would roam over Europe, Asia and Africa as a cow and would finally rest in Egypt where she would be turned back into a woman and that one of her descendants would release Hercules. Again he hints about Zeus and she exits in a frenzy.

Wow! That was a long one!

THIRD STASIMON (lines 887 - 907)

The Chorus prays that a god would never woo them and that it is best for one to marry one's own kind.

EXODUS (lines 908 - 1093)

Prom continues to be defiant. Hermes arrives having been told of Prom's hints about Zeus and demands to know the full story. Prom still defiant accuses Hermes that he's no more than a gofer and lackey for Zeus and refuses to spill the beans. Hermes warns him that Zeus will send an eagle to devour his liver daily. Prom sticks to his principles and indignantly and stubbornly remains defiant. A storm comes over with thunder and lightning. The rock is struck and the earth opens up and Prom disappears.

Oh, Boy! How do you interpret all that particularly when the other two plays of the trilogy are lost?

The moral of the story is ..... "don't get your father angry at you because he may put you out of the house and you may turn into a cow." But seriously now. Aeschylus was a conservative kind of guy. If he lived today, he'd be definitely a Republican. He felt that you should negotiate and not go to extremes. Not like Zeus and Prom both of whom were stubborn as a mule and unyielding. I mean what if the eagle finally decided to have some other parts - a steady diet of liver gets kind of boring.

Aeschylus presents several conflicts here and moralises like all good religious thinkers do. Unyielding authority vs progress, rebellious reform vs tyranny, reason vs force. The timelessness of his themes should be apparent to anyone holding a PhD from Harvard. Can authority be merciful and just? Can people respect it unless it is? Can force and wisdom compromise? Can we have bacon and eggs for breakfast?

Aeschylus believes that life is tragic, a far cry from the excesses of the 80s. Suffering is inevitable but must be endured and we become wise through suffering. We must have personal responsibility for sin. The cure is moderation. He couldn't have been a fun guy to be with. Most fun people I know don't even know the word moderation. He also believed that authority must be wise and humane to be respected. He was a dreamer too. I don't know of any authority that has been both wise and humane in the last 2500 years. Do you?

But let us move on to the only existing complete trilogy - the ORESTEIA - composed of three plays - as all trilogies are - Agamemnon, Choephoroe and Eumenides.

AGAMEMNON

AGA for short.

Unfortunately, you'll need some background here. And if you think that Prometheus was hard to pronounce, wait till you see some of the names here. Tongue twisters at best. Who but a Greek would ever dream up a name like Clytemnestra?- CLEE-TEM-NEE'-STRA. Even if you did, would you name your daughter like that? Today we'll shorten it and call her say Cly as in Sly. Back to the background however.

King Atreus - not such a prince of a man - had a spat with his brother Thyestes. So what do you suppose he did. He killed Thyestes' two children and fed them to him as .... lunch. (Wonder what recipe he used.) Thyestes was fuming. I'd say he was reasonably justified because he did not like stew at all, particularly all that garlic. So he in turn killed his brother Atreus. Agamemnon, Atreus' boy, gets upset, even though he becomes King and kills his uncle. (So far it sounds lilke a Friday the 13th movie.) Orestis, Electra, Iphigenia and Chrysothemis - see what I told you about tongue twisters? - are Agamemnon and Clytemnistras' kids. From now on we will call them Ore, Eli, Iphi, Chryssie , Aga and Cly. It just happened that at the time, the Greeks had to conquer Troy because Paris of Troy had hurt their pride by eloping with Helen, the wife of Menelaus, who was Aga's younger brother. There was no wind though. What to do? They talked it over and decided the easiest way to get the wind to sail to Troy would be - can you believe that? - to sacrifice Aga's daughter Iphi. Cly - and I don't blame her for this - never forgave Aga for it. During his ten years' absence she had a thing going - a tryst you know, like Erik and Sheila in" The Young and the Restless" , with Aegisthus the son of Thyestes who escaped his brother's meals. Cly feels vey guilty with three kids around and a lover and what have you, so she sends Ore away on vacation and plans to do away with Aga when he returns.

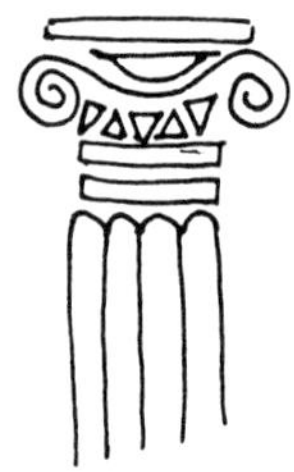

CHARACTERS

Watchman	
Clytemnestra	wife of Agamemnon
Herald	
Agamemnon himself	the King of Mycenae
Aegistus	Cly's lover, son of Thyestes
Cassandra	daughter of King Priam of Troy, sister of Paris who eloped with Helen. Agamemnon's captive. She was also a Prophetess (with Tarot cards and all) (I like that name)
Chorus of Elders	

PLOT

PROLOGUE (lines 1 - 39)

Scene - Agamemnon's Palace. Cly has assigned a well-paid watchman to sit on the roof and watch for the fire that would signal the fall of Troy and the return of Aga. What a job that must have been! Well, civil service jobs haven't really changed much since then. After several months of inactivity, day dreaming and reading everything he could get his hands on, the watchman sees the light. He is joyous. Finally he gets to come down from the damn roof and get a change in assignment. At the same time he is fearful not knowing what in the world is going to happen when Aga returns with Cly and Aegistus and all that.

PARODOS AND FIRST STASIMON (lines 40 - 269)

A Chorus of Elders enters. They are elders as they were old enough ten years before not to have gone to Troy to fight for revenge. Cly prays, and well she should, by an altar.

The Chorus tells us of the omen before the war predicting destruction. Two eagles killing a rabbit. It sounds like a bad dream. Calchas the soothsayer isn't so soothing. He prays to Artemis and Apollo, predicts the destruction of Troy by Agamemnon and Menelaus, but also sees future woes. The Chorus now prays to Zeus' benevolent side. He punishes men for their sins regardless of his benevolence and teaches them how to become wise through suffering.

Agamemnon, ambitious to become a great conqueror and avenge his brother, had gathered the forces at Aulis and just for the heck of it sacrificed a sacred animal. Wrong. Artemis the protectress of animals and president of the local SPCA, was peeved and ordered the winds to stop to spite Aga. Calchas, the not-so-soothing soothsayer, ordered Aga to sacrifice Iphi his daughter. Aga said "Wait a minute, Calchas. You are talking about my daughter, and I love her." And Calchas answered "Well Aga, if you want the winds to start, you gotta do it or else you'll sit here forever and you know how much of a drain on your budget it is to feed all these troops." Aga's ambition got the best of him, and despite Iphi's pleas, her father sacrifices her anyway and the winds start blowing - which makes a lot of sense. I bet you couldn't do that today and get away with it. But eventually justice prevails and Aga will get his.

FIRST EPISODE (lines 270 - 366)

Cly announces the fall of Troy and exalts the merits of technology and how they got the message speedily by starting consecutive fires on mountain tops over 800 miles. She is sure the Trojans will suffer and suggests that the homecoming of the victors would be perilous. She had something in mind for Aga you see.

SECOND STASIMON (lines 367-480)

Sin is punishable and the whole city of Troy is punished for the sin of Paris. Is that fair? Well that's the way it is. You got to pay the piper. Don't do the crime if you can't do the time! The gods have a little note pad and jot down all those who commit sins and punish them. Religion has not really changed that much after all these years, has it? Also there are statements that imply that too much fame is dangerous. We all know that. After all, look at what happened to the likes of King Tut, Napoleon, Madonna, Michael Jackson .

SECOND EPISODE (lines 481 - 685)

After several days have passed, the Chorus doubts Cly's story about the fire and all and about technology. But a herald arrives, really happy to be home after ten years overseas and announces that Aga is coming soon but Menelaus is delayed because of a storm. The Chorus hints at the difficulties at home and the herald tells of the suffering of the army with all that waiting and the budget cuts. Cly proclaims her undying love for Aga and her fidelity over the years. Little Liar!!!

THIRD STASIMON (lines 686 - 773)

Helen, that wench brought misery to all around her, except Paris of course and that was just in the beginning when they were really infatuated with one another. The Trojans in the beginning thought that she was quite the catch and were happy and proud that one of their boys got her. Soon though they changed their tune.

Was a little pride really worth ten years of misery and starvation? And in all reality only Paris had some fun. You see when good fortune comes from evil deeds it is inevitable that it brings disaster. Look at Al Capone for example. Pride and arrogance bring retribution. We all know that, yet we continue being both proud and arrogant. Will we ever learn? Humility is best. But then again I like Frank Lloyd Wright's statement "I prefer honest arrogance to hypocritical humility."

THIRD EPISODE (lines 774 - 965)

The hero Aga arrives on a chariot followed by Cassandra, his captive, sister of Paris and Prophetess and lover. What is a man supposed to do ten years away from his wife? A little fling or two never hurt anybody. Aga thanks the Gods and says he'll put order to the State again. Cly dublicitous as ever declares her undying love for her hero and tells him that she sent Ore away for safekeeping. Then she asks him into the palace on a purple carpet she spread out just for him - special - Agamemnon greets Cly coldly - not even a hug after all these years. He does not want to tempt the Gods with pride as though he had never done it before. But she insists and he yields like any good husband should, takes his shoes off and walks on the purple carpet, not neglecting to turn over his paramour and captive, Cassandra, to Cly's care. A lot of nerve the guy had.

FOURTH STASIMON (lines 966 - 1018)

A gloomy Chorus fearful of woes to come despite the .... red carpet homecoming ceremonies.

FOURTH EPISODE (lines 1019 - 1410)

Cly emerges from the palace and asks Cass to come in. Cass does not respond till after Cly has re-entered the palace. Then she has a fit. Woe, alas, alack and all that.

Poor me, in the hands of these horrible people. She, being a prophetess herself, predicts Aga's murder and her own giving a detailed account. The Chorus does not believe her. Why should they? She continues to rant and rave incomprehensibly mixing past crimes with ugly prediction of the future including Orestes' revenge once he finds out that she and Aga were done in. With resignation though she finally enters the palace. What else could she have done?

Agamemnon's death screams are heard. The Chorus moves about in great concern. Cly, holding a bloody axe, appears and happily and triumphantly announces that she has done away with Aga and Cass.

EXODUS (lines 1411 - 1673)

Cly asserts herself and tells all . She killed Aga and Cass, she had no remorse and she was happy about it. After all Aga had sacrificed their daughter, had carried on with Cass and scores of other women and she truly loved Aegisthus. Besides there was a family curse and what is a mother to do?

Aegi comes in as cocky as can be with his bodyguard and boasts about his part in the scheme, and his affair with Cly. Not only that but he and Cly will rule from now on. Quite the opportunist the man was.

The Chorus hopes that Orestes will avenge the death of his father. Cly and Aegi proclaim that severe measures will be taken in the kingdom. Eric tells Sheila that he can't marry her until after the fall show. Sheila is disappointed. Stephanie is still hoping. Oops, that's from another story. Sorry.

CHOEPHOROE

(HO-EE-FO'-REE)

LIBATION BEARERS

LIBATION = WINE OFFERING TO A GOD

Several years later Orestes returns with his buddy Pylades-Pyl's the nickname. Apollo has ordered him to avenge his father's death. (This was a nice and short background.They should all be like it.)

CHARACTERS

Orestes	son of Aga and Cly
Pylades	Ore's pal
Electra	Ore's sister
Clytemnestra	Aegisthus' wife
Servant	
Aegisthus	Cly's hubby
Chorus of maidens	

PROLOGUE (lines 1 - 21)

Orestes in disguise enters with his friend Pylades and walks to his father's tomb and lays a lock of his hair on it.
A cry of woe is heard from the palace. The Chorus enters with Electra - Ele- as the two retire. Cly has sent them to the tomb to make offerings as she had had nightmares all night and could not sleep.

PARODOS (lines 22 - 82)

The Chorus wails and wails and wails ad nauseum. (Too much wailing isn't good for you.) Cly still cannot sleep. The Chorus have been sent to placate Aga's soul, but his soul is unplacatable (bet you didn't know such a word existed, did you?) However, murder cannot go unpunished and justice is inescapable. You just don't sweep things under the rug that easily.

FIRST EPISODE (lines 83 - 304)

Sad confused innocent young Ele doesn't feel like praying for her mother Cly. Would you? The Chorus urge her to pray instead for the return of Ore and to face revenge. Ele finds the lock of Ore's hair on the tomb and recognizes that it looked just like hers before Lady Clairol. So Ore must be back.

The Chorus is still wailing and lamenting. This is getting insufferable. Then Ele sees footprints that look like hers. At that very moving moment, Ore walks in and the two embrace. Ore then prays to Zeus for protection, and well he should, and reveals to Ele that the oracle of Apollo ordered him to take revenge for their father's death.

FIRST STASIMON (lines 305 - 476)

They all kneel at the tomb of Aga. The Chorus, Ele and Ore chant laments over Aga's death, over his greatness and promise vengeance. Ore becomes decisive and is supported by the no longer sweet and innocent Ele.

SECOND EPISODE (lines 477 - 582)

Determined and strong after the inspiring event by their dad's grave, they pray for guidance and assistance. The Chorus tell Ore of his mother's nightmare and sleepless nights which strengthens his determination, and he reveals his scheme to do away with Cly and Aegi.

SECOND STASIMON (lines 583 - 648)

A woman's passion is the most monstrous thing on earth and makes her commit untold crimes. Cly proves just that. Justice will prevail as it always does in cowboy movies.

THIRD EPISODE (lines 649-778)

The plan is set into action. Ore and Ply present themselves to the palace and ask for hospitality. Cly with Ele welcome them (if she only knew!). Ore tells them that he is a messenger from Phokis and he was sent to tell them of Ore's death. (What a liar!) Cly is happy as a cat purring but doesn't show it, and sends Ore's old babysitter (nurse) to summon Aegi to hear the good news. The Chorus, fans of Ore, tell the nurse to suggest to Aegi not to bring his bodygard.

THIRD STASIMON (lines 779 - 836)

The Chorus wants no mercy for Cly and Aegi and prays that the scheme will be carried out to perfection.

FOURTH EPISODE (lines 837 - 933)

Aegi becomes a little sceptical about Ore's death and enters the palace. His death screams are heard. A servant tells Cly of Aegis' fate and when Ore and Pyl appear, she pleads for mercy. Ore hesitates a bit but good old Pyl, always a trusted friend, reminds him of Apollo's edict. Without pity, he drags his mom into the palace and slays her next to Aegi.

FOURTH STASIMON (lines 934 - 970)

We are delivered from evil (Where have I heard this one before ?) and justice has indeed triumphed.

EXODOS (lines 971-1074)

Cly's and Aegis' bodies are seen through the doors covered with the robe that Aga wore when he was done in. Now that is a nice little touch. Who would ever have thought of it! Ore shows the corpses and tells why he did it. He goes berserk and tells everyone that Apollo made him do it. Where do you suppose Flip Wilson got his "The devil made me do it" line? See, there's nothing new under the sun.

The Furies (his conscience) begin to haunt him. Why, did he think he was going to get off scot free?

EUMENIDES

Pronounce this as you wish, but the closest Greek way I can come up with is EV-MEH-NEE'-THIS

The Furies, agitated and irritated over Ore killing his mom pursue him relentlessly, not only that, but also continuously. Mad, Ore runs for protection to the Temple of Apollo. (A short and sweet background again.)

CHARACTERS

Apollo	A god
Apollo's priestess	
Orestes	Cly's boy
Clytemnestra's ghost	Ore's mom
Athena	A goddess
Twelve citizens of Athens	

Chorus of Furies (horrific minor divinities who go after sinners)

PLOT

PROLOGUE (lines 1 - 63)

Apollo's priestess is praying standing before his temple at Delphi. As she enters the temple and sees Ore bloodstained and the Furies surrounding him, she quickly exits in horror as though bit by a rattlesnake.

FIRST EPISODE (lines 64 - 142)

Inside the temple, Apollo reassures Ore that he will not desert him and tells him to go to Athens and ask Athena for help. "The Furies are just nasty. Just don't pay attention to them, Ore," he said. Hermes is leading Ore away but the Ghost of Cly appears and tells the Furies off for sleeping, so they slowly awake.

FIRST STASIMON (lines 143 - 178)

The Chorus - the Furies in other words this time - rebuke Apollo and promise him that Ore will not get away with it.

SECOND EPISODE (lines 179 - 243)

Apollo drives the Furies out of his temple, but they defend their haunting of Ore and tell Apollo that he's doing nothing less than protecting a mother killer. Apollo tells them that it served her right and she had it coming because she had killed Ore's dad. The Chorus pledges that they will continue relentlessly their pursuit of Ore. Poor boy. Back to Athens. Ore praying for deliverance more than for forgiveness clings onto Athena's statue as though it was his mother's skirt.

PARODOS (lines 244-275)

The Furies (Chorus), looking for Ore, locate him and pledge vengeance.

SECOND EPISODE CONTINUED (lines 276 - 306)

Ore pleads for help and claims to have atoned for his sin. The Furies tell him that there's no way out of it.

SECOND STASIMON (lines 307 - 395)

The Chorus (Furies) proclaim their function to avenge unpunished crimes. After all, Fate gave them that assignment. How would Apollo dare to interfere! They are the powers of darkness and their job is to punish the guilty. That's why all men fear them.

THIRD EPISODE (lines 396 - 489)

Athena enters the scene or the proscenion to be exact. (You hadn't already forgotten the proscenion now, had you?) Questioning the Chorus, she finds out that Ore had not quite been a nice boy. Ore pleads with Athena that Apollo made him do it - the same old defense - and that he had cleansed himself already. Athena's verdict is that since there seems to be some justice on both sides as well as some injustice on both sides she'll have the case tried before a panel of judges. Fair enough?

THIRD STASIMON (lines 490 - 565)

It makes sense that if Orestes is acquitted others may follow his example and kill their mother if their mother had killed their father. Then crime will triumph. So we must have some authority which we must fear (or else would we all be criminals?) The key word is MODERATION. And killing your mother is not a very moderate thing to do. You are evil. And those who are evil must perish.

FOURTH EPISODE (lines 566 - 776)

Athena, the Goddess of Wisdom, enters along with twelve moderate Athenians. In those days apparently there were moderate Athenians. Apollo is the defense attorney. After all, he was the one who made him do it and the least he can do is defend him. The Furies are his prosecutors. Ore admits that he killed his mother but says that Apollo made him do it. He doesn't change his tune. Apollo defends Ore by saying the real order came from up above, from Zeus in other words. How many times have you heard that one before? "I was just following orders." Then they argue as a Greek can only do so well as to which is the greater crime, as though there is an answer. Is the murder of the husband by the wife better or worse a crime than the murder of the mother by the son? Athena as a judge instructs the jury that they must reach a decision. Alas, the vote is a tie: a hung jury. Athena then casts the deciding vote for acquittal. Joy of joys. Ore leaves proclaiming he loves everybody.

FOURTH STASIMON (lines 777 - 792)

The Furies, bad losers that they are, dislike the younger gods and their rising power. They threaten sanctions against Athens.

FIFTH EPISODE (lines 793 - 915)

Athena tries to pacify the Furies that are going wild, wailing and wailing, telling them that actually it all came from Zeus, who is nowhere to be seen, as is the case with most important Gods. They are invisible. She even promises them honors and a nice new home in Athens. Now this is bribery but what can you do? She begs and begs and they finally say "What the heck, we got a new home, after all."

EXODOS (lines 916 - 1047)

The Chorus (Furies) having ensured a new home for themselves have now changed their tune and pray for continuing blessings for Athens. That's how the custom of bearing gifts was started. Athena on the other hand continues to pat them on the back by telling them how important they will be. A large procession of Athenians led by Athena their protectress,chant in joy and lead the Furies, who by now are given a new name Eumenides (the Kind Ones), to their new home which is a cave with wall to wall carpeting and indoor plumbing, and all's well that ends well.

NOTES & COMMENTS

For those of you that do not have a PhD from Harvard or even from UCLA, the trilogy is easier to interpret than Prometheus Bound because it is complete.

There are several morals that come from it. First of all, you can commit a crime and get away with it if you convince the jury or the police that the devil made you do it. It is still true today. If your attorney convinces the jury that you were not in possession of your faculties - mentally incompetent they call it - you can get off scot free or just by spending a little time at a mental institution where the doctors keep you there till they are convinced that you no longer hear those nasty little voices inside your head.

Another moral is that punishment is inevitable and that it is the only supreme justice.

We learn a lot about ourselves through suffering. That's how we become wise. (Then all these unwise people around us must have never suffered.)

Too much of a good thing may be wonderful but moderation is best.

Evil breeds evil.

Finally, you can be forgiven for your sins by Zeus. (Now we have Christ.) And Zeus, Athena, etc. are forces of light and they are better and they control the forces of darkness (the Furies) ..... by bribing them.

Aeschylus introduced the idea of judgement by one's peers rather than by priests, VIPs or Kings. I'm not sure if that was a good idea. Look where it has gotten us. Our prisons are overflowing. I guess we haven't bribed the Furies enough.

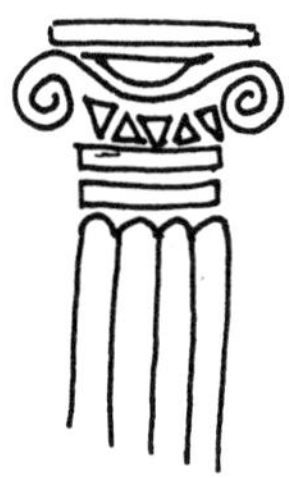

B - SOPHOCLES

SOPHOCLES 497 - 405 BC

So - fo - cles (much easier)

Sophocles lived a long time, wrote an estimated 125 plays and was the most popular and successful playwright and poet. He added a third actor, increased the dialogue, tempered the Chorus and introduced scene painting. His trilogies are an organic unit rather then a serialized theme.

Existing plays

Oedipus Rex
Philoctetes
Women of Trachis
Electra
Oedipus at Colonus
Antigone
Ajax

Sophocles' plays are more complex and intricately and skillfully constructed. His characters, sharply contrasted, undergo changes through crises and events and these are attributed to character flaws which lead to inevitable suffering and unexpected disaster which must be endured. Certain idealism - people as they should be - permeates his work. He uses dramatic irony masterfully. Do you know what that is? It really isn't much different than regular irony, just placed in drama therefore "dramatic".See? Despite imperfections, there is a dignity in man. Moderation is still the central theme of Sophocles and reverence towards the Gods. Pride and arrogance lead to disaster. Wisdom comes to us through suffering just as Aeschylus said. (I wish it wasn't true.) The Gods willl punish us (they still do), we will suffer and only then may we become humble and realize our limitations.

Four of the existing plays will be described , reviewed and properly "fractured" here (leaving three for the next book).

OEDIPUS REX

Here's where you'll learn who Oedipus (E-dee-pus) was. Laius (LA-EE-US) and Jocasta were the happy King and Queen of Thebes until one day the oracle at Delphi predicted that they would have a son, who under normal circumstances ought to bring joy to a household. Not to theirs though, because their son, Oedipus, will kill his father and marry his mother (that way his sister would be his daughter and his son his brother). I wonder if the writer of modern soaps got some ideas from Sophocles.

The child was born and indeed it was a boy.

To make sure that the prophecy of the oracle wouldn't come true, the unproud parents gave it to a shepherd to kill. The shepherd went to it by first piercing the baby's feet for some strange reason. When the baby started crying, not being accustomed to having his feet pierced, the shepherd, instead of killing it, gave it to another shepherd from Corinth to kill. Eventually the good-looking child was adopted by Polibus and Merope who happened to be King and Queen of Corinth as luck would have it. When Oedipus grew up, he learned about the prophecy and didn't like it one bit. He left Delphi - that's where the most famous Oracle was-determined never to return there to avoid the unpleasantries. He got on his Ferrari Chariot but unfortunately at a spot where the three roads met, his chariot was blocked by another chariot. You see even in those days Greeks were notoriously poor chariot drivers. In the unavoidable argument between the two Greek drivers, the hot-tempered Oedipus lost it and killed the other driver, a common occurrance not only in Athens today but also in Los Angeles. Irony of ironies, it was his father Laius!! Fleeing on his delux chariot, he reached Thebes of course unaware whom he had killed. Had he found out it would 've ruined the rest of the story.

Unfortunately, right before the city, the Sphinx, an ugly monster who spoke Greek, would not allow anyone to enter the city unless they answered a riddle. If they didn't, unmercifully she would kill them. You can well imagine that not too many tourists went to Thebes in those days. Oedipus, sharp as a tack, answered the riddle and the Sphynx destroyed herself in despair. Oedipus was an instant hero with the Thebans because now they could build hotels and restaurants and everything. Such a hero he was that everybody wanted him King and since Laius was dead all he had to do is marry his widow (his mother Jocasta) and he did. But they did not live happily ever after. Well, they did have four kids - Antigone, Ismene, Eteocles and Polynices - and he did rule fairly and justly and was admired for his wisdom until one dark day a plague struck the city and people were dying right, left and centre.

CHARACTERS

Oedipus	King of Thebes
Creon	Oedipus' uncle, Jocasta's brother but also his brother-in-law
Jocasta	Queen of Thebes, Oedipus' mother but also his wife
Priest	
Teiresias -	blind soothsayer

Messenger from Corinth
Shepherd
Second Messenger
Chorus of Theban Elders

PLOT

PROLOGUE (lines 1 - 150)

Oedipus enters and the priest tells him about the plague that's killing everybody and their brother. The priest begs Oedipus to do the same thing with the plague as he had done with the Sphynx, as though they were one and the same thing. Oedipus reassures him that Creon had gone to Delphi to find out what to do and that he should be coming back soon. In comes Creon, happy as a lark because the cause of the plague was revealed to him by the Oracle. All they have to do is find out who killed Laius because he is still in the city and either kill him or banish him. Oedipus finds out that the only witness to the killing reported that it was a band of thieves that had done Laius in. So Oedipus decides to play detective and find out as soon as possible who the murderers were.

PARODOS (lines 151 - 215)

The Chorus prays to as many Gods as they can remember to deliver the city from the pestilence.

FIRST EPISODE (lines 216 - 462)

Oedipus issues a proclamation ordering the culprit to come forth or else he will be denounced. He tells everyone that

down and to think rationally. He tells Oedi that never had he been that ambitious and that he was saying all these nasty things because he was angry. In comes Jocasta, trying to be the peace-maker. She tells Oedipus that the old man couldn't be right because Laius was supposed to have been killed by their son, not a group of thieves. Moreover the boy was killed right after he was born.

When Oedipus hears where Laius was killed, he remembers that he had killed a man at that spot. He is horrified and he suspects that he is the murderer of Laius and orders the witness to come forth. Oedipus tells of his past in Corinth and the fantastical prediction of the Oracle that he would slay his father and marry his mother. Resolving never to return to Corinth is his roamings, he had killed a man at the crossroads. Jocasta, however, the faithful wife and mother, somehow convinces him that all this is circumstantial evidence and coincidence and the old man is not to be trusted.

SECOND STASIMON (lines 911 - 1185)

The Chorus' confidence in the Oracle is shaken. Prosperity is no good. Reverence for the Gods is best. (Very much against the values of the 1980s where you can't be too rich or too thin.)

THIRD EPISODE (lines 911 - 1185)

Jocasta prays to Apollo and a messenger enters from Corinth, announcing Polybus' death. Jocasta is tickled pink and calls Oedipus to tell him the great news that proves that the Oracle is dead wrong. Oedipus is elated, but the messenger also reveals that Polybus was not his real father anyway. This messenger knows a whole bunch. When Oedipus questions him further, he reveals that the baby Oedipus was given to the messenger by a shepherd from Laius' household, the same shepherd who coincidentally witnessed the murder. The plot thickens. Jocasta realises what's happening and tries to convince Oedipus to leave it alone. Knowing his determination, however, she runs into the palace in agony.

The Chorus though is elated that Oedipus is from Thebes - as for the rest - a minor detail.

The poor shepherd is ushered in. With the Corinthian messenger standing by, Oedipus relentlessly questions him and runs into the palace in horror. (What would you have done in those circumstances?)

THIRD STASIMON (lines 1223 - 1530)

Life is a bitch and then you die. Now you know where this profound diction came from.

OEDIPUS AT COLONUS

Twenty years after the tragic events - the latter ones not the earlier ones - we find the exiled man, Oedipus, a wreck of a man, a beggar being taken care of by Antigone, his daughter. Meanwhile, back in Thebes, Eteocles is the King and has banished his brother, Polynices, (a lot of trouble in that family) who went to Argus and organized a whole expedition against Thebes to seize the Kingdom. He is ready to attack, but another Oracle tells the Thebans that if they want the city to prosper, they must bury Oedipus there.

CHARACTERS

Oedipus	
Antigone	his daughter & sister
Ismene	his daughter & sister also
Theseus	King of Attica
Creon	Oedipus' uncle and brother-in-law
Polynices	Oedipus' son & brother
Messenger	
Native of Colonus	
Chorus	Elders of Colonus

PLOT

PROLOGUE (lines 1 - 116)

The blinded Oedipus arrives at Colonus with Antigone on his side only to be told that he is in the sacred forbidden ground of the Eumenides. Remember them? They are the rehabilitated Furies. Oedipus prays to them for help and deliverance.

PARODOS (lines 117 - 257)

The Chorus enters looking for the stranger who's tresspassing. Oedipus comes forward and the Chorus is shocked by his appearance. They tell him to get out of there and then ask him who he is. Reluctantly, he tells them, and in horror they ask him to leave immediately. Fortunately, they express some pity for the two as well.

FIRST EPISODE (lines 258 - 667)

Oedipus, or Oedi or Edie, momentarily gains some of his old dash and convinces the Chorus to grant him asylum and wait for King Thesus. Instead, suddenly, Isme, his daughter, comes in and Oedi and Anti hug and kiss her. Oedie asks Isme about the two boys, his sons, and whatever happened to them. They don't even pick up the

murder and incest and all that stuff. Why even support him? Oedi, emotionally says that he hadn't done any of those things knowingly so maybe he was not guilty. So Thes, siding still with Oedi despite all his bad luck, forces Creon to lead him to rescue the two girls. It's kind of nice to have friends like Thes, don't you think?

THIRD STASIMON (lines 1044 - 1095)

The Chorus back in contact with reality foresee the combat between Thes and Creon and pray to Zeus, Athena, but also Apollo for their King. (The more the Gods, the merrier.)

THIRD EPISODE (lines 1096 - 1210)

Anti and Isme come back with Thes to Oedi. There is joy and hugging and kissing and much happiness, and Oedi thanks Thes, who tells Oedi that some relative wants to talk to him. Somehow Oedi knows it is his son Poly and he simply refuses to see him, but Anti again says "Oh com'on daddy, don't be so cruel. He is not only your son, but also your brother." What else could Oedi do but give in?

THIRD STASIMON (lines 1211 - 1250)

The Chorus sings the merits of a short pleasant life because old age only brings grief and sadness and much suffering. I mean look at Oedi. There's a prime example for you that can drive you to suicide in your early thirties.

FOURTH EPISODE (lines 1251 - 1555)

In comes Poly, takes a long look at the sad-looking pair - his father and sister - tells them how sorry he is things did not quite turn out for them, but maybe there's luck in the near future if they help him against Ete, and reminds them of the Oracle's latest hallucinations. But Oedi is unforgiving and tells Poly in a stirring passionate speech "What do you want from me you no good SOB after you let me rot for twenty years? Get out of my sight. Hope both of you guys drop dead!" which is not a very nice thing to say to your son if he is your brother or to your brother even if he is your son. Before leaving though, Poly begs his sisters to give him a decent burial if he doesn't come up on top in his scheme against Thebes.

The Chorus once again remind us of the woes of Oedi and how life patterns keeps on repeating themselves as we hear thunder. Oedi feels kind of insecure, down right unsafe somehow, so he calls Thes who comes promptly. Oedi tells him that he feels his time has come and soon he will tell him where he willl die, something that only the Kings of Athens should know and protect because it will protect Athens from Theban aggression. Divinely he is slowly led to the fated spot where he is to die.

ANTIGONE

But the show must go on. Polynices led the expedition against Thebes. It was known as SEVEN AGAINST THEBES, something like the MAGNIFICENT SEVEN with Yul Brynner. Well, Poly wanted to be King and he didn't want his brother Ete to have the throne. The war went on and on and everybody got tired of it all and said "How about you two guys dueling it out and whoever wins gets the throne. What's the sense of having armies fighting, cities under siege, people starving, sanctions carried on and all the like. You guys want it, you two guys fight over it and leave us alone." That makes a lot of sense to me. Wish they did it nowadays.

Unfortunately, in the fight there was no survivor. The two brothers killed each other. What a sad fate this family had! Creon becomes King, buries Ete with honors for defending Thebes, but does not bury Poly at all because he was a traitor. And if anyone tries to bury him, they will be punished by death. Not a good prospect.

CHARACTERS

Antigone	daughter of Oedipus & sister
Ismene	daughter of Oedipus & sister
Teiresias	blind soothsayer
Creon	King of Thebes
Eurydice	his wife and Queen
Haemon	their son
Guard	
Messengers	
Chorus of Elders of Thebes	

PLOT

PROLOGUE (lines 1 - 99)

The two sisters Anti and Isme are in front of Creon's palace. Anti is strong headed and determined to bury her brother Poly despite Creon's decree. Isme is a shy, timid and quiet little girl and tries to dissuade her sister, telling her she must obey the state. Anti's going to do it even if it costs her her life and is contemptuous of Isme's shy retreating ways.

PARODOS (lines 100 - 162)

The Chorus celebrates the liberation of Thebes and the defeat of the traitor Poly (the earliest form of the soft shoe dance known).

FIRST EPISODE (lines 163 - 331)

King Creon, arrogant as can be, declares the State supreme above all, and repeats his decree not to bury the traitor brother Poly whose body is being guarded to prevent burial. I don't know how long this went on, because eventually the guards themselves wouldn't be able to take the stench.

having to do with her family's bad luck. The Chorus sympathises with her but tells her that fair is fair. She did it and she caused her own downfall.

FOURTH EPISODE (lines 883 - 943)

A very short episode because Creon doesn't want too much fuss or mess and just wants Anti entombed alive and the whole thing over with. Anti, on the other hand, bids adieu to the city and its people.

FOURTH STASIMON (lines 944 - 987)

The Chorus reminisce of other unfortunate souls that have suffered in the past.

FIFTH EPISODE (lines 988 - 1114)

A boy leads the blind soothsayer Teiresias in. Teir, always an optimist and a gem of a fellow even if he is blind, warns Creon that the Gods are angry because Poly's corpse is lying there unburied and the city is being polluted. (He should see it now!) He warns him also that he is being too stubborn and inconsiderate, thinking only of himself. This angers Creon a lot and he accuses the old soothsayer of taking bribes to bring about Anti's release. This really angers Teir (there was an awful lot of anger and gnashing of teeth and other parts of the body going on) who says that Creon will pay for not burying Poly and for doing away with Anti, by losing his son Haem. Now you'd expect Creon to really see red. Not here. Creon starts wondering what if the old man is right. Can he take his chances? Better not. So he renegs and he is off to release Anti and bury Poly.

FIFTH STASIMON (lines 1115 - 1152)

The Chorus in glee sing to Dionysus who is the God protector of Thebes.

EXODOS (lines 1153 - 1353)

A messenger arrives and tells Eurydice, Creon's wife, who finally comes on stage in a cameo part, how wonderful a burial Creon gave to Poly. Then he went to release Anti and found her hanging and very dead and his boy Haem crying bitter tears. A destitude Haem unsuccessully tried to kill his dad and then successfully committed suicide with his sword while hugging Anti's body.

A broken remorseful man, Creon comes in with Haem's body in his arms. To make matters worse, a messenger comes in and tells of Eurydice's suicide over her son's (Haem's) suicide. In utter misery, understandably, Creon prays for his own death.

PLOT

PROLOGUE (lines 1 - 120)

Ore, Pyl and the valet enter the stage (orchestra). The old man explains that they are in front of the royal palace. Ore shrewdly orders the old man to go into the palace and gauge the situation by telling them that Ore is dead. Meanwhile, he and Pyl will pay a visit to Aga's tomb and then come back with an urn that supposedly contains Ore's ashes. They're off conveniently as Electra enters crying and carrying on over Aga's death and her own tough luck, dead father, brother away and a mother who has a lover and is paying no attention to her but insults, degrades and belittles her all the time. (Reminds me of my ex-wife.) She's very lonely and becoming despondent.

PARODOS (lines 121 - 250)

The Chorus commiserates with Electra, they condemn murder and urge her to stop feeling down because ..... life goes on. They tell her that they too hope that Ore'll be back but it is up to Zeus who makes all those decisions. Electra cannot forget or forgive the murderers and dwells on her misfortune, living in squalor, without a husband even though she used to be quite attractive. She's searching for a way to punish the murderers and is totally consumed by the whole idea.

FIRST EPISODE (lines 251 - 471)

Electra tells of her unfortunate lot, her misery and her general depression, while Cly and Aegi live happily as King and Queen. Is this justice for murderers? Does crime pay? Does she have to endure Cly and Aegi's mental cruelty? The Chorus tries to comfort her and make her feel better by telling her that Ore'll surely be back. Chrysothemis - Chrys to us - enters and agrees with Electra's charges but pleads with her sister to just give up, submit to the rulers. In one ear and out the other,in other words, to maintain some semblance of sanity.

Electra, being a fighter, rebukes her sister for being a coward. Then Chrys tells her that unless she shapes up, Aegi will put her in a dungeon as he has threatened.

Then she continues gossiping a bit about their mother and the horrible dreams that she (the mother) had been having and the fact that she poured - Cly that is - libations on poor Aegi's tomb.

Electra and the Chorus gang up on her and persuade her to substitute a lock of Electra's hair and one of her own as offerings to Aga. Strange habits these people had.

FIRST STASIMON (lines 472 - 515)

The dream means that Justice will triumph in the end for the house of Atreus which had had many woes.

and caution but urges Ore and Pyl not to waste time and act at once. They enter the palace.

THIRD STASIMON (lines 1384 - 1397)

Aha! Finally , sweet revenge. Rejoice!

EXODOS (lines 1398 - 1510)

Electra's looking for Aegi. Cly's cries are heard as are her pleas for pity and forgiveness. Ore and Pyl come out and proudly report Cly's death. As Aegi approaches, the two re-enter the palace. Aegi orders the gates opened and Ore and Pyl are standing by a covered thing that looks like a corpse. Thinking still that it must be Ore's body, Aegi is overjoyed. In horror though, he realizes that it is Cly not Ore, as he lifts the cover. Ore takes him inside to kill him at the same spot where his father was slain. Whew! What a story!

MORAL OF THE STORY

Some murders are OK. (Cly's and Aegi's) Today they are called "justifiable homicides".

Punishment of the guilty reconciles conflicts and Justice thusly triumphs.

SOME NOTES ON STYLE AND TECHNIQUE

Complex plots - with three actors and more dialogue than before with diminishing importance of the Chorus. Character development through experience and sudden events. His style is graceful and lucidly simple and dignified.

Sophocles had orthodox religious views so if there's conflict in human or divine purposes, the Gods reign. Humans, because of character flaws, fall from grace and inevitably suffer. Even if you don't deserve it, if you're human you must suffer.Once again I don't like that one, one bit.

Arrogance, pride and sin lead to disaster and punishment. I don't like this one either because some sin I like very much.

However, the central theme of moderation and wisdom through suffering isn't all that bad and we all know that suffering really makes one know onself better than joy does. Oh well, I wish it was the other way around, but it ain't. And Sophocles says so too.

TROJAN WOMEN

The title pretty much betrays what the whole thing is about. Troy has just fallen after years and years under seige through the clever wooden horse ploy.

Let me refresh your memory quickly. The Greeks could not capture Troy and reclaim their lost pride by taking back Helen. So they built a huge wooden horse inside which a bunch of soldiers hid. They gave it to the Trojans as a ..... gift for their fighting spirit. The Trojans rejoiced and immediately took the horse within the walls of the city and started frolicking. After frolicking a lot, people usually want to take a good nap. That's what the Greeks took advantage of, got off their wooden horse, opened the gates so that the rest of them could enter and literally caught the poor Trojans with their pants down. The Trojans did not like to fight with their pants down and half asleep. The Greeks took over the city , herded the Trojan women into huts in front of the walls and merrily set Troy on fire.

CHARACTERS

Athena	Goddess of wisdom and defense
Poseidon	God of the sea
Hecuba	old Queen of Troy
Cassandra	(still like that name) Hecuba's daughter, a prophetess but also a little nuts
Helen	Menelaus' ex-wife
Menelaus	King of Sparta
Andromache	Hector's wife
Talthybius	Greek herald

Chorus of captive Trojan women

PLOT

PROLOGUE (lines 1 - 152)

As the play opens we see Poseidon, who was not only the God of the sea but had also helped build Troy and was protecting it, lamenting the destruction of Troy. He feels really bad because the captured Trojan women will soon be apportioned to the Greeks. Such was the custom of the day. To the victor belong the spoils you know. It still is the custom in wars, only we don't like to admit it. At least the ancieny people were honest.

PARODOS (lines 153 - 234)

The Tojan women are not really looking forward to their captivity. The Greeks have been fighting for years and you know their reputation anyway. They are slave drivers, regardless of whether you're a slave or not.

FIRST EPISODE (lines 235 - 510)

Talthybius - let's call him Tal - enters and gives the women their assignments as to who they are to serve. Cassandra goes to Agamemnon. She was beautiful. Hecuba's ugly daughter, Polyxena, will be sacrificed at Achille's tomb. Andromache, Hector's wife - Hector is dead by the way - will be given as a concubine to Achille's son and Hecuba herself to Odysseus. Now this is what I call revenge. Hecuba, having heard many stories about Odysseus, is very much afraid for her future.

Tal calls Cassandra - Cass to us. For some reason she is in a great mood - remember she's got a screw loose and maybe she liked sex a lot - and is holding a torch like the Statue of Liberty. She's singing, making up songs about her future with Aga. Hecuba calms her down and predicts Aga's death, or wishes him dead. Cass switches her tune and raves madly about Aga's and Odysseus' future miseries and bad fortune. Now Tal tries to calm her down. After she bids farewell to her mother, she leaves for Aga's ship.

Hec is still lamenting her own fate. Now at this age she ought to be a woman of leisure not some Greek's concubine and slave. I mean she had been a Queen you know. The fact that she has lost her husband and sons bother her too as does her separation from her friends and family.

FIRST STASIMON (lines 511 - 576)

The Chorus recalls the story of the wooden horse and how the Trojans fell for it, unfortunately.

SECOND EPISODE (lines 577 - 798)

Andromache - Andro - Hecuba's daughter-in-law, enters with Astyanax her son in her arms. Both women mourn a bit more over their fate. Hec laments the death of Polyxena but Andro envies her because she herself would rather be dead than a slave not to mention a concubine. Hec tries to comfort her by telling her to raise her son Asty(anax) to avenge his ancestors.

Tal returns and sorrowfully reports that it was decided to throw the boy off of the walls to make sure that no avenger grows up. Bravely Andro hands over her son to Tal after a tender if pathetic farewell speech.

SECOND STASIMON (lines 799 - 859)

The Chorus laments the fact that in the past Troy used to be a favourite of the Gods but recently they didn't - the Gods that is-seem to love the Trojans any more because this was the second time in recent memory that they - the Gods again - allowed the city to be captured. There's an awful lot of lamenting and bewailing in this tragedy, don't you think? After all, lifes does go on and it behooves one to make the best of it, be it as a slave or a master.

THIRD EPISODE (lines 860 - 1059)

Menelaus gloats over the recapture of his beloved Helen who is being held as a slave with the rest of the Trojan women. He calls for her and Hec - there's no love lost there - urges him to have no mercy or pity on her. Menelaus threatens to kill her but Helen begs. She wants to tell her side of the story, which predictably is that she really didn't want to go with handsome young Paris, but he forced her and abducted her and you know what. What could she have done, a weak powerless creature that she was. Hec calls her (Helen that is) a liar and tells Menelaus that she was very happy and infatuated with Paris in Troy. Menelaus wants to kill Helen right there and then as he is convinced that she's lying. After all, Paris was his guest. But a fool that he is for beauty, like all men, just looking at her,he melts and allows her to be taken back to Sparta . He'll decide later how to... punish her. A real sucker, Menelaus was.

THIRD STASIMON (lines 1060 - 1122)

Everybody abandons Troy. Men and children have been killed. The Gods have abandoned Troy as well. Only the women are left to suffer

EXODUS (lines 1123 - 1332)

Tal enters holding Asty's body. Andro has sailed away he says and asks Hec to bury her grandchild quickly. Hec mourns again over her grandson whom she places on Hector's shield to be buried.

The Chorus mourn again as Asty was the last hope for Troy.

Tal orders the women to get ready to sail. Hec has an urge to leap into the flames of the city instead of going with the Greeks. The Chorus laments once again and so does Hec who prays to her dead.

The city walls topple in flames and the women turn toward the ships.

THE MORAL OF THE STORY

Euripides may be the first pacifist in history. The play was written during the Peloponnesian War which was a war between Athens and Sparta. Euripides condemns war as a futile folly in which humans engage from time to time, that destroys both victors and vanquished. Yet, having learned nothing from the past, we still to date, engage in this barbaric ritual.

MEDEA

Jason, the great old adventurer, has been looking for ..... the golden fleece. Aren't we all? Good luck, Jason. Well, anyway, at Colchis, Medea falls madly in love with him. Head over heels. She happened to be the King's daughter no less and besides that she was a sourceress as well. A mighty dangerous combination. Medea decides to help Jason in his dangerous task. To be able to get away with her love, she kills her own brother. See what love can do? Not only that, but she also does away with Jason's uncle as well. He was a treacherous old soul anyway. Banished, Jason and Medea find sanctuary in Corinth where, as nothing had ever happened, they live in bliss for ten years and have two sons besides. But soon there are clouds in this idyllic romance. Creon, the King of Corinth, offers his daughter to Jason, in marriage that is. What is a man supposed to do if he wants to be King? He accepts the offer. But ..... obviously there is more to this story. Read on.

CHARACTERS

Medea	Jason's divorced wife
Creon	King of Corinth
Jason	Medea's ex and a golden fleece opportunist
Aegeus	King of Athens
Nurse	of Jason and Medea's little ones
Guardian	of Jason and Medea's children (we are talking about real influence here)
Messenger	
Chorus of Corinthian Women	

PLOT

PROLOGUE (lines 1 - 130)

The nurse wishes that Jason had never come to Colchis because that was the beginning of a chain of events that were not all that happy. First of all of course was Medea's obsessive love for Jason, followed by her two murders. And now Jason abandons her to marry the princess of

Corinth and that has made Medea both physicallyCorinth and that has made Medea both physically and mentally ill - severely depressed - and who knows what she is capable of doing now! Of course, she kind of feels bad for doing away with her brother and Jason's uncle but she did that for love. Imagine what she can do for hate and revenge! The guardian comes in with the two boys and brings more bad news: Creon, to be on the safe side, is about to banish Medea and the boys. The news shock the nurse. Just in case, she's going to keep the boys away from their mother. We then hear Medea's voice lamenting her fate and the nurse speaking about wisdom and moderation.

PARODOS (lines 131 - 213)

The Chorus asks the nurse about Medea whose voice is still lamenting, threatening vengeance and praying for death all at the same time. The Chorus tries to be understanding and to comfort her and counsels her to be patient. The nurse then describes Medea's very strong fierce personality, makes a comment or two on how sad life is and then kind of suggests that music brings comfort, an out of the clear blue piece of advice.

FIRST EPISODE (lines 214 - 409)

Medea, a veritable mad woman by now, after all that bewailing and lamenting, enters recounting her problems and the fact that she's an immigrant there. Then she switches to her married life and all her sorrows as a wife and the sorrows of all married women and promises to find some way to avenge herself. She sounds like a very early feminist to me.

Creon enters and orders her and the boys out of his Kingdom immediately because he has heard her threats and he knows that a woman scorned has no equal in planning nasty things for others. But Medea begs to be allowed to stay in peace and that she's powerless to do anything nasty. Creon is smart though and he won't be dissuaded. He's also stubborn, so Medea asks him for just one day to pack her things and what have you. The moment Creon is gone though, she reveals to the Chorus that she just needed one day to put into action her fiendish scheme of revenge, not giving a darn about the consequences. Not only that but she didn't care either.

FIRST STASIMON (lines 410 - 445)

The Chorus tells of the changing world and how old ideas are being cast aside and how women are becoming more and more important in society. (Boy, it's taken a long time - isn't that what the ERA-Equal Rights Amendment- is about?) The Chorus also tells of Medea's independence and vitality. She's not about to obey a King's orders just because he's a man. She'll do her own thing.

SECOND EPISODE (lines 446 - 626)

Jason enters and tells Medea that she has brought everything upon herself by constantly bewailing and lamenting and threatening, but he offers her money to take care of her and the boys and the nurse and the guardian and generally keep herself in the style she was accustomed. But Medea will hear none of this alimony balony and lets Jason have it with a barage of unflattering epithets about how unjust he is and about her being homeless. Jason peevishly says that he's doing it all for his sons and ..... family and dares to tell her that she's selfish and obsessed by jealousy. Who wouldn't be, Jason? Come on now. Medea then calls him a liar and tells him that his real reason was ambition and that he married the princess secretly and that she's much younger than herself and that she wants to have nothing to do with him or his money and to please leave her alone. A regular ex-husband ex-wife quarrel, wouldn't you say? Kramer vs Kramer of old. So Jason leaves her alone to manage for herself,to pay for the nurse and the guardian and the cook and the gardener e.t.c.

SECOND STASIMON (lines 627 - 662)

The Chorus preaches that obsessive love is harmful, and that moderation is best, and exile a horrible thing.

THIRD EPISODE

Aegeus, the King of Athens, is passing through Corinth on a little pleasure trip and he meets Medea who asks him for asylum in Athens. Unaware of her nasty plans, Aegeus says OK, why not? Medea puts the finishing touches on her plot. She's going to pretend that she's reconciled with the whole idea of Jason marrying a younger woman and everything is wonderful. Then she's going to send the new wife poisoned gifts, using her sons as bearers so nobody will suspect anything and that will not only do her in but also all those who touch her. Then she'll kill her own kids so that Jason will feel bad. Altogether a pretty nasty scheme, wouldn't you say?

THIRD STASIMON (lilnes 824 - 865)

How can a mother do such a nasty thing? And how can Athens, such a blessed city, receive such a murderess the Chorus asks.

FOURTH EPISODE (lines 866 - 975)

Medea begs Jason's forgiveness as he enters and tells him that she now fully understands his motives. Jason's happy as a lark about it all. Medea asks Jason to talk to Creon so that the boys at least can stay near him in Corinth and sends a robe and a diadem (both poisoned) with the boys to Jason's young new wife. (Now, how one can poison either a robe or a diadem, I do not know.)

FOURTH STASIMON (lines 976 - 1001)

The Chorus feels bad about the children who,unbeknown to them, will be accomplices to a crime. They also feel bad about Medea who will murder her own kids.

FIFTH EPISODE (lines 1002 - 1250)

The guardian reports to Medea that Creon had a change of heart and the boys can stay in Corinth. Medea now has a very serious conflict within herself. She's torn between her love for her kids and her desire to kill them so that Jason will feel bad. At first her love overwhelms her but finally her hatred wins and she decides to follow her initial plans. At least nobody can accuse her of not having some second thoughts.

FIFTH STASIMON (lines 1251 - 1292)

The Chorus finds that women are seldom wise, that people without children do not know what a lifelong responsibility it is to have children and that having children is not always what it is cracked up to be.

EXODOS (lines 1293 - 1419)

The messenger reports in grim detail the deaths of the princes and King Creon who hugged his daughter while she was in the throngs of the poisoned robe and crown and died himself. Determined then, she rushes in to carry out the last grim part of her scheme and we hear the cries of the children. The Chorus of course condemns Medea's actions. (Does this sound like a Friday the Thirteenth movie?) Jason rushes in to rescue his children but he hears that it's already too late. Medea miraculously appears above the house in a dragon drawn chariot. Jason regrets ever meeting such a nasty person and bemoans his bad luck. Who wouldn't? He begs for the bodies of his kids to bury them. Nasty to the very end, Medea denies his request, takes off in her chariot with the kids' bodies and leaves Jason a broken man.

THE MORAL OF THE STORY

Mothers shouldn't kill their children. Seriously though, Euripides' character study of a person whose love turns to hate and desire for revenge, presents internal conflicts and uncontrolled emotions of anger and jealousy and love. Unresolved they can bring disaster. He also creates sympathy for women who suffer greatly and are considered inferiors under (ancient) Greek marriage customs. So how much of this has changed in the past 2500 years? What's new? Once again the timelessness of the Ancient Greek writers comes to the forefront. The real sense of the tragic is that after all these years little if anything has changed. We keep on doing the very same things.

HIPPOLYTUS

This play I swear, is what the soap opera artists of today read and have created zillions of variations of. This too is a story about love. Hippolytus - Hip to us - is Theseus' son. Theseus is the King of Athens and had a thing going with Antiope, an Amazon Queen. This Amazon Queen was not from the Amazon River but was an Amazon - in other words, a LARGE lady.

Hip is a hunter. He just loves it and doesn't much care to fool around with the ladies. Thes, his father, married a young Cretan princess, Phaedra, and has several kids with her one after the other. Upon casting eyes on Hip, Phaedra falls madly in love with the handsome younger man who is also about her own age. But she is a married woman, you know and she is good and virtuous even if she is a little weak and no matter what, Hip will never know. Continued next week.

CHARACTERS

Hippolytus	the illegitimate son of Theseus
Phaedra (Fe-dra)	wife of Theseus
Theseus	King of Athens and Troezen
Aphrodite	Goddess of Love
Artemis	Goddess of the Hunt
Hip's pal	
Phaedra's nurse	
Old Hunter	
Chorus of Hunters	
Chorus of Women from Troezen (Tree-z'in)	

PLOT

PROLOGUE (lines 1 - 120)

Aphrodite is angry because Hip ignores her worship and instead worships Artemis, so she must punish him. (See, the Greek Gods were jealous too, no different than the people.) Being a Goddess, she knows things that humans don't, so being the Goddess of Love she knows about Phaedra's passion for Hip. Even if she's the Love Goddess, she ..... hates people who don't worship her. She vows to make Theseus learn about Phaedra's passion for his son and then Hip and Phaedra can ..... die and everything will be well and good with her.

Hip enters with a bunch of hunter friends and praises Artemis. Hip not only praises Artemis but he also places a wreath at her altar and boasts how pure he is. An old hunter with life experiences that only age brings, warns Hip not to be so cocky and to fool around with women because he is young and not fooling around with women at that age might be considered irreverent toward Aphrodite. She may be the Goddess of Love but who knows what she's capable of, if you're irreverent.

PARODOS (lines 121 - 175)

The Chorus tries to guess why poor Phaedra is ill. Maybe she is insane, or maybe her husband Theseus loves another woman, or maybe there are problems in Phaedra's family, or maybe she's going to have another baby, or maybe she ran out of cornflakes for breakfast.

FIRST EPISODE (lines 176-524)

The nurse and Phaedra enter with the nurse deeply concerned over Phaedra's illness. In the midst of her suffering and fever, Phaedra's only concern are her looks, so besides everything else she suffers from an acute case of vanity as well. Almost in a trance, Phaedra hates being the wife of a King and with oodles of responsibilities and kids and a palace to take care of and she'd rather be off in the woods or in the mountains. Suddenly she realizes that she's dreaming of being in the same place as Hip. She's consumed by utter shame because she had dirty thoughts and wishes to die. (What else, I mean how else would we have a tragedy unless every time somebody thinks something nasty then they wish to die and soon they do.)

The poor nurse tries to console Phaedra and tells her how much she cares for her and ..... (what else) advises moderation. (See the classic writers even 2500 years ago knew that Greeks are people of extremes and made their morality plays advising moderation and temperence and patience - to no avail of course. To date we're still people of extremes.) The nurse asks Phaedra where it hurts but Phaedra won't say a word. The poor nurse, not knowing what else to do or to say, tells Phaedra that if she doesn't take care of herself and dies her children will suffer or even be harmed because Hip will succeed Thes to the throne. At the very mention of his name, Phaedra falls apart and goes into a tizzy. The nurse is no dummy and suspects something going on and asks many questions till Phaedra finally confesses her undying passionate love for Hip. Phaedra somehow calms down having confessed and gotten it off her chest. She talks about how difficult it is to be virtuous and how ashamed she is to have those secret impassioned thoughts for Hip, and adds that she hates unfaithful wives that drag the family honor through the gutter. Honor is more important than happiness. The nurse is very understanding but does not agree.(Neither do I.) She wants to see her lady happy and uses all kinds of arguments to change her mind and give in to her passion and save her life. Phaedra seems to weaken a bit but the conflict between love and honor is very strong. Oh, if we could have both!

FIRST STASIMON (lines 525 - 564)

How strong Love (Eros - Cupid) really is! Even Zeus the King of the Gods and Hercules the strongest of all were overwhelmed by Eros and had several extra-marital affairs.

SECOND EPISODE (lines 565 - 731)

The nurse, overwhelmed by love and devotion for her mistress, approaches Hip herself. Being a wise old nurse, she makes Hip take an oath that he'll never tell anyone what she will tell him and then goes on to speak of Phaedra's passionate desire for him. Hip of course is shocked and he'll have nothing to do with the whole thing.

Not only that, but he'll tell Theseus his dad. The nurse reminds him "Hey boy, you've taken an oath, remember?" but under the circumstances Hip does not feel that he ought to keep the oath. I mean, this is really serious stuff. Are we going to worry about a little oath? He pushes the nurse aside and in front of Phaedra, he has a fit screaming and yelling that women are the root of all evil. (Who gave the apple to Adam? Do you have any doubts now?) As soon as Hip leaves, Phaedra tears into the old nurse who's trying to defend herself by arguing that she did it all because she wanted to see Phaedra happy and nothing else and had she not failed, Phaedra would not be treating her like this.

Unfortunately, Hip's rejection injured poor Phaedra's pride and vanity so much that now she.... hates him. Sort of sour grapes attitude. Now she's sure that the only way to save her honor and her name is to punish Hip. So she's simply going to kill herself and take Hip down with her somehow. Hell hath no fury .....

THIRD EPISODE (lines 776 - 1101)

Phaedra did it. She hung herself. As Thes arrives from a journey anxious to see his family, he discovers his wife's death. There's a lot of lamenting and bewailing and just then he notices a note tied to Phaedra's hand. It's her suicide note. Phaedra says that she did it because Hip had ..... violated her against her will. (Maybe Hip is right after all.) Furious, Thes prays to Poseidon to grant him one of the three wishes and kill Hip instantly, and just in case that doesn't happen, he orders him banished just to make sure.

Hip comes in to greet his dad and sees Phaedra's corpse. At first, nobody will answer his questions as to what has happened. But then Thes attacks him for being nasty, corrupt, dishonest and dishonorable and hiding all that under the pretence of purity and chastity and besides that he is also a hypocrite and a very bad boy. Calling him names, he banishes him right there and then, again.

Hip defends himself by saying "Hey, everybody knows how pure and good and honest and honorable I have been and I still am." As much as he wants to tell all, his honor will not let him because of his oath to the nurse. Then he dares speak about his own birth. How could Thes accuse others when he himself had ravished his mother out of wedlock at that. Thes in a rage banishes him again and again. Hip says farewell and leaves. What else could he do?

THIRD STASIMON (lines 1102 - 1150)

Oh if we can only find happiness. Life's full of suffering and unexpected turns. Poor Poor Hip.

EXODOS (lines 1151 - 1466)

Hip's friend enters and tells in full detail of an accident that has mortally wounded Hip. As he was leaving on his chariot, big waves frightened his horses. Well it was both the waves and a sea monster that Poseidon had sent. The chariot was upset and Hip was hurt as a result. Thes asks to see his son. The Chorus speaks of Aphrodite's success in punishing Hip and out of the clear blue, Artemis appears above the palace on a cloud and reveals to Thes the whole truth and tells him off to boot for not believing the honorable and pure Hip, who's being brought in at the moment and thus he has a chance to converse with Artemis whom he adores. Wow! Of course, good old Artemis tries to make him feel better on his deathbed and vows to take revenge from Aphrodite by someday doing away with one of her devotees. (She does.)

Hip, the nice young man that he was, forgives his father, who's beyond himself now, embraces him and dies promptly.

THE MORAL OF THE STORY IS THAT

it doesn't pay to be virtuous and good. That's how some of the Greeks interpreted the death of Hip. However, the scholars and academicians tell me that this is not the case and that what Euripides is trying to bring forth is the conflict which is created at times when the conventional standards set up by society clash with our desire for personal happiness or gratification. Or between sex and chastity as I see it. Euripides advocates that pride, jealousy, anger and vanity overcome reason. And they shouldn't. Uncontrolled emotions and human weaknesses can cause tragedy, he warns. We also see a not so subtle criticism - if not attack - on jealous and vindictive gods or the religion of the day - gods who remain in conflict while humans reconcile.

And of course the everpresent moderation and temperence. Oh, if the Greeks had listened!

ELECTRA

SETTING

Cly and Aegi (no need to talk about them again as we've done so many times before) have married off Electra to a peasant in an attempt to humble if not humiliate her and to prevent the noble birth of a child who might want to avenge Aga's murderers.

CHARACTERS

Electra	daughter of Aga and Cly
Orestes	son of Aga and Cly
Cly	Aegi's wife, Aga's widow
Pylades	Ore's friend
Peasant	Electra's husband
Dioscuri	Castor and Pollux's Gods
Old man	
Messenger	
Chorus of Peasant Women	

PLOT

PROLOGUE (lines 1 - 167)

Electra's peasant husband in front of his hut recounts Aga's murder by his wife Cly and her lover Aegi and that Ore's been sent away and Aegi's got a price on Ore's head just in case. The peasant husband swears that he's so overwhelmed by Electra and respects her position that he cannot bring himself to touch her so the marriage has not been consumated. Why that is important I will never know.

Electra enters in rags bringing water and explains why she's the way she is, apologetically.

The two take off and Ore and his pal Pyl enter. Ore explains that his task is to avenge his father's death as has been ordered by the Oracle of Apollo. All he has to do is kill Aga's murderers and then they can be off and running again. Now he must look for his sister Electra. She returns from the water-well mumbling something about Aga's loss and Ore's absence so many years.

PARODOS (lines 168 - 212)

The Chorus of peasant women announce a sacrifice to

Hera, Zeus' wife, and tell all the women of the area to participate. Electra politely declines because she's very unhappy and besides she's got nothing to wear. The Chorus, being peasant women, in vain try to comfort her.

FIRST EPISODE (lines 213 - 431)

Ore and Pyl come out of hiding and Ore tells Electra, who doesn't recognize him because so many years have passed, that Ore's alive and well and that the peasant husband really respects her. I'm not sure how the conversation could drift so easily from one thing to another like that, but nothing is strange in Greece, even in those days.

Anyway, Electra hopes that Ore will return andl help her to kill their mother and her lover. Electra then tells Ore, still not knowing who he is - she sure is a trusting soul - of how humiliated she feels being a peasant and not a princess any more, that her mother and Aegi are now governing over Aga's Kingdom, that Aegi has no respect for Aga's grave and of his mockery of an avenger.

At that very moment, the peasant husband enters and politely welcomes the strangers and invites them into his humble hut. Ore, impressed, concludes that a good man, a virtuous man, is not so because of birth but rather because of character. Electra then sends her husband for Aga's foster father to help in entertaining the guests.

FIRST STASIMON (lines 4321 - 486)

(Let me remind the reader that Euripides really de-emphasized the Chorus to the point where their comments are almost totally irrelevant.)

Achilles went to Troy dressed in a gorgeous armour, but Aga the commander-in-chief was murdered by his wife. And vengeance is coming. Now if that makes any sense to you it's fine, because it makes no sense to me. I simply must report it as this is what the text says.

SECOND EPISODE (lines 487 - 698)

An old man comes in with food for the strangers. No sooner does he deliver it, than he starts crying over evidence of new sacrifices on Aga's tomb, which is no way to entertain guests, but what can you do? He also says that he has found locks of hair which means that Ore must be back. Electra says "Come on old man. This is absurd. You can't tell by hair or footprints because we don't have the forensic means yet." (Euripides here is discrediting his predecessors Aeschylus and Sophocles on the recognition scenes.)

Ore and Pyl come out of the hut and the old man recognizes Ore by a scar on his forehead which is a real sign, not footprints and hair. Electra and Ore embrace each other and the Chorus rejoices. In all this glee, Ore asks how he is to murder his mother and the old man explains and not only that, but they plot to murder Aegi at a coming sacrificial feast. Meanwhile, Electra will lie to her mother Cly, telling her she's got a son. Cly will come to the hut and that'll be all. A weak Ore plans to kill himself if the scheme fails but headstrong Electra assures him it won't. How could it?

SECOND STASIMON (lines 699 - 746)

Pan gave Atreus a golden lamb for his flock, but his wife was in love with his brother Thyestes. The two conspired and Thyestes got both the animal and the throne of Mycenae. When Atreus discovered all this, he went berserk and committed atrocious crimes. Because of it, Zeus transformed all Nature, yet Cly slew her husband, which has nothing to do with the rest of this, but the Chorus has got to say something.

THIRD EPISODE (lines 747 - 1152)

A messenger tells Electra, in great detail, that Aegi not knowing of course that the strangers were Ore and Pyl, offered them his hospitallity and that Ore had taken care of Aegi with an axe as Aegi was performing a sacrifice himself. Things went as planned so Electra and the Chorus rejoice as Ore and Pyl come in with Aegi's body. Electra tells all the evil deeds of Aegi, kicks him and hides the body in the hut.

At the sign of Cly, Ore weakens again, thinking that after all it is his mother he's to kill and you don't do such a thing easily and Apollo must be cruel to want him to do that. Electra encourages her brother. She isn't going to do it, Ore is. No skin off her back.

Cly arrives and immediately defends herself and her murder of Aga. Guilty conscience you see. Electra says "Baloney mother, you and Aegi were carrying on, that's why you killed poor old dad." Cly's motherly instincts come forth and she feels remorse for having treated her daughter so badly, particularly now that Electra has made her a grandmother. Electra finds the opportunity right then to ask Cly to go in the hut for the necessary purification rituals. Cly accepts and Electra rejoices once again. Everything's going as planned.

THIRD STASIMON (lines 1153 - 1182)

Justice is about to be done. Hurrah!

EXODOS (lines 1183 - 1359)

Cly's dying cries are heard from the hut. After the fact,

Ore and Electra are overcome by serious remorse, noble souls that they were.

They worry about their future blaming Apollo for the horrible deed.

Lo and behold, what to do? How to resolve this? Deus ex machina of course.

Castor and Pollux, the Dioscuri appear above and reveal that Cly had it coming anyway but Apollo was not lily-white either. They order Ore to marry off Electra to his pal Pyl. Poor peasant. He got shafted in the deal, gentle soul that he was. Ore will be pursued by the Furies (his conscience in other words) but will be formally acquitted after a trial in Athens and everything will be peachy-creamy. Cly's and Aegi's bodies should be given proper burial.

Ore regrets his parting with Electra again so soon after they had finally gotten together but what can you do? So he bids a warm au revoir to his sister and leaves. The Dioscuri meanwhile warn all against the treacheries of injustice.

THE MORAL OF THE STORY

Don't kill your mother if you don't want your conscience to bother you and above all don't expect the Dioscuri to appear and save you.

This is truly a psychological drama of the tortured souls of Electra and Ore but mostly Electra and her strengths and weaknesses.

A FEW NOTES ABOUT EURIPIDES' STYLE, TECHNIQUE AND PHILOSOPHIES

Unlike his predecessors, Euripides uses complex plots and suspense. The Epilogues include resolution of conflicts via the deus ex machina ploy. The Chorus part is of little importance or totally irrelevant, almost a musical intermission.

What interests Euripides is the human character,human emotions and conflicts within oneself or between his characters. He is the one that introduced the theme of love in drama and gave special importance to female characters. He used clear, simple everyday language with great lyric beauty, but also formal rhetorical eloquence.

Euripides was very interested in political, social and religious matters. He criticized the orthodox religion and also the conventional social standards with rational liberalism.

His existing plays are on three basic themes: religion, women and war. He sees no reason for war and hates violence. He criticizes the double standards of women and tries to elevate their lot.

Although not an atheist, he criticizes the evils of religion such as oracles, soothsayers and the like and sympathises with all human suffering brought about by the clash of emotions, of reason and emotion and of absolute standards and morals.

III

COMEDY
ARISTOPHANES

Tragedy is a goat song as I explained earlier. Well. Comedy is also a song, the song of Komos. What is "Komos" you ask? Komos is the choral element which originated in the fertility ceremonies at the festival of Dionysus or the ribald revelry and frolicking in his honor. Comedy thus is replete with frank indecency, obsenity some call it, especially in regards to sex. Reality is suspended in order to make a satirical point on contemporary issues, be it that they are political, social or moral. Could be compared to a Gilbert and Sullivan musical comedy.

Comedy was produced at the Dionysia, following tragedies. The Chorus wore fantastically incredible costumes and there were 24 of them. The actors wore masks and sandals (and costumes as well, I presume). There were also contests among three poets, each of them presenting one comedy.

Comedy had a slightly different structure than tragedy. It was divided into the following five parts:

I	Prologue - the protagonist conceives a brilliant idea.
II	Parodos - the Chorus enters
III	Agon - a debate takes place between the proponents of the idea and the opposition, which inevitably loses out

IV Parabasis - the Chorus speaks to the audience, stating the poets' views

V Episodes - the idea is put into use

ARISTOPHANES OF ATHENS

about 446 - 385 BC

Little is known about Aristophanes other than the fact that he was a very funny man. So funny, that he makes you cry. He is considered the greatest comedy writer. He wrote most of his plays during the Peloponnesian War. Of his estimated 40 works, only 11 survive today. They are:

- Acharnians
- Birds
- Clouds
- Ecclesiazusae
- Frogs
- Knights
- Lysistrata
- Peace
- Plutus
- Thesmophoriazusae
- Wasps

As to the pronunciation of some of them, forget it. There is no way that anyone in his right mind would even attempt it. And why should they? Unless you really want to sound intellectual at some time or another and out of the clear blue you start talking about the satirical impact of The-smo-fo-ria-zoo-seh in today's context.

I wanted to do Lysistrata, as it is one of the juiciest and sexiest of all. Instead, I decided just to tempt you with this because I want tol include Lysistrata in my next book. Tricky don't you think? So we'll start with BIRDS. See how wrong you are? No, it was neither Daphne du Maurier nor Alfred Hitchcock that thought of it first. It was Aristophanes.

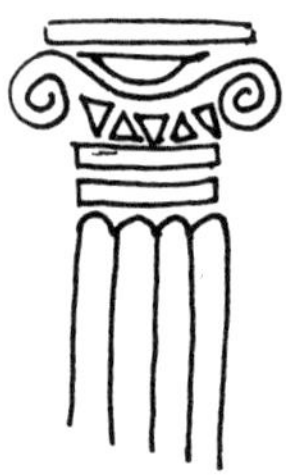

This is nice. No Background here.

BIRDS

CHARACTERS

Euelpides (Ev-el-pi`-des)	an Athenian
Pisthetaerus (Pis-the-te`-rus)	an old Athenian rogue
Epops	a bird
Prometheus	a Titan
Poseidon	God of the Sea
Heracles	a hero and now a minor God
Chorus of Birds	

PLOT

PROLOGUE (lines 1 - 259)

Pisthetaerus - Pist.(I had trouble with this one) - and Eue appear in a desolate godforsaken area with a bird in hand each. The birds are their guide to the Kingdom of the Birds. Good thinking boys! The two friends have left Athens for a quieter more peaceful city, just like many Athenians are still trying to do today. But they are discouraged because they can't find any place to suit them. They call Epops and when he finally appears, they explain what they are up to and they want his advice on the matter. He makes several suggestions, but they reject them all. Out of the clear blue, Pist has a great idea. Why don't the birds build their own country between the earth and the heavens? This way they'll be able to intercept the smoke from the sacrifices made by humans to their gods and they'll be masters of men and gods alike. Epops gets really excited at the prospect and calls his wife and a bunch of other birds. (Wife's name is Procne!)

PARODOS (lines 260 - 450)

The Chorus - all birds - come in one at a time. Pist and Eue comment with some allusions on contemporary VIPs. The Chorus asks why they have been summoned, look over the two men suspiciously and are ready to peck them to death. (Daphne's idea for The Birds.) Epops stops them just short and asks the two Athenians to explain their ingenious scheme to the birds.

AGON (lines 451 - 675)

Pist and Eue start to do a selling job for their project to the birds. They tell them that after all the birds were the first creatures on the earth and were once the rulers of all lands. Then they tell them how important birds are to men. Having flattered the birds enough, they propose the building of a city between earth and heaven. When the city is finished, the birds can send an ultimatum to the gods and to men, demanding loyalty from the gods and worship from men, as the birds are superior to both. The birds are very impressed by the scheme. They love the idea of being the masters of the universe and go for it.

PARABASIS (lines 676 - 800)

The Chorus moves forward and speaks to the audience giving them a lecture on the origin of birds and how important they are to men, and invite them to come to live with them and enjoy a life free of legal restrictions as in Athens. And finally they tell of the advantage of having wings and how wonderful it is to fly anywhere they wish

.

EPISODE (lines 801 - 1057)

Pist and Eue return. Somehow they have sprouted wings, they decide to name the new country Cloudcuckooland and they supervise its construction. They also compose prayers to the new bird-gods.

A great number of impostors arrive, such as a poet, a propher with his oracles, a government inspector general, and a mathematician, but they're all rejected. They wanted new blood, not the same old stuff!

SECOND PARABASIS (lines 1058 - 1117)

The birds proclaim that they are divine and issue decrees and penalties for those who injure birds in any way. They talk about their carefree happiness and award prizes for the best play in the current competition to them, of course who else, offering blessings.

EPISODE (lines 1118 - 1705)

One messenger tells of the wall of the city erected by the birds and another messenger announces that a wayward god, Iris the messenger of the Gods, has entered the new city. The arrogance of the birds shocks her. Pist threatens the gods with an all out war, closing the city to them and ordering all the smoke from the sacrifices to be intercepted. The expression "holy smokes" must have come from this.

Prom, of old, comes hiding under an ..... umbrella so Zeus cannot see him and wearing a mask just to make sure. He reveals that the gods are starving and a big feud has started between the Olympian and the foreign gods. He then advises Pist that when the gods send them peace negotiators, he should demand the scepter of Zeus as a token of submission and the hand of Basileia (Ba - si-li'a) -

royalty- in marriage. She's Zeus' housekeeper. Now that's total control!

Poseidon, Heracles and a foreign god arrive as peace envoys from the gods. Pist states his terms. The negotiations are long and drawn out. Heracles is offered dinner which not only pacifies him, but also apparently wins him over to the side of the birds and he votes to accept the terms. Poseidon casts a dissenting vote and the foreign god talks gibberish, which is interpreted by Pist and Heracles to mean that he is voting for peace and the birds' terms. Agreement is reached, all the terms accepted, and the preparations for Pist's wedding to Basileia are being made.

EXODOS (lines 1706 - 1765)

The blessed day is finally here. Pist and Basileia enter with Pist having Zeus' thunderbolt and lightning in hand. As the Chorus of birds sing hymns of adoration to them and wedding marches, the happy couple fly off to Zeus' palace where they are going to sit happily and reign over gods and man, which is finally a happy ending fit for a Hollywood production instead of the bloodbaths of tragedy.
(Please note that in COMEDY there has been a change in format, just to make things a bit more interesting)

CLOUDS

Again no background!!! Rejoice! Comedy's more fun!

CHARACTERS

Socrates	Athenian philosopher, headmaster of the school "Thinkery"
Strepsiades-Stre-psi-ades	Athenian gentleman
Phidippides- Fee-dee-pee-dis	his son with a holein his pocket.

A servant
Unjust Cause
Just Cause
Money Lender X
Money Lender Y
Chorus of Clouds

PLOT

PROLOGUE (1-262)

Strep is tossing and turning in his bed, unable to get any rest worrying about his son's debts. The boy Phi, is hooked on betting in chariot races and even talks in his sleep about the races. Strep can't sleep and recalls how all his troubles started when he married a high class city lady. Their first quarrel was over the boy's name. The wife insisted that there was some reference to a horse. And of course she won as Phidippides means a Horse Sparer's son. (Please, don't ask me what a Horse Sparer is.) So the boy grew up with a passion for horses. What can one do? That's when Strep comes up with a brilliant idea, he thinks. He wakes his son up and pleads with him to enrol in Socrates' school and learn how to argue in court and win the lawsuits that inevitably will come from people wanting to collect their debts. His hope is that clever arguments will help him in evading payment. Phi refuses to go to school though, because it will interfere with his ..... tan. Strep decides to enrol himself despite his old age. What the heck, it couldn't hurt! See, parents had problems with their kids way back then.

As he knocks on the Thinkery's door, he is told off by one of Socrates' disciples for disturbing his studies. He is anxious though to enrol and he sees a number of students studying a variety of subjects. He finally locates the master himself suspended in a basket from the roof. Surprised, he hears that the master himself cannot think unless he is in a rarefied atmosphere. Strep tells Socrates why he wants to enrol in his school.

PARODOS (lines 263 - 509)

Socrates prays to the Clouds, to Ether and Air. The Chorus of Clouds enters and frightens Strep with their song and dance. He is told however that these are the Goddesses who inspire tricky oratory and help impostors and quacks. Socrates tells Strep about the Clouds and their power and also that there is no Zeus. According to Socrates, Zeus has nothing to do with rain and thunder and lightning. The Clouds control all that. And right he was! Strep is amazed and convinced and swears by Chaos, the Clouds and the Tongue as the only Gods, and he is ready to discipline himself and work hard to learn enough eloquent tricks to outwit his creditors. Socrates gives him a qualifying exam in which Strep reveals that he is primarily interested in evading the debts. Soon they enter the Thinkery.

FIRST PARABASIS (lines 510 - 888)

Socrates is upset over Strep's bad memory and stupidity. Strep enters and is asked to lie on a bed as Socrates instructs him. Bet you thought it was Freud who first had the idea. Not so. It is obvious that the old man doesn't give a hoot about learning for its own sake but learning just what is necessary to evade his debtors and his main interest is the art of false reasoning. After an unsuccessful session in the gender of nouns, Strep is told just to lie in bed and ponder, but he is attacked by bed bugs and screams in pain. Finally, he reveals to Socrates that the only thing he can think about is how to outwit his creditors. Socrates is thoroughly disgusted with the old man and dismisses him from his school because of his bad memory.

Strep, disappointed, decides that either Phi enrols in the school or he's going to kick him out of the house. He then tries to teach Phi some of the tricks, but Phi thinks it's a bunch of phooey. He enrols in the school, however, as he doesn't want to be thrown out of the house.

FIRST AGON (lines 889 - 1112)

Phi is instructed by Just Cause and Unjust Cause. Just Cause stands for truth, justice and honesty. Unjust Cause, on the other hand, stands for material success. The two argue and quarrel with each other. Finally they give their summation speeches. Just Cause speaks of the old school which teaches honesty, justice, discipline, modesty, good health, physical exercise and fitness, morality and good manners, patience and respect for elders. Unjust Cause presents the thought of the new school which teaches ways to find loopholes in the laws, win arguments through clever speaking - never mind truth and accuracy - how to talk yourself out of a difficult situation, and how good it is to take hot baths, and be sexually loose. Just Cause loses on a ...... technicality and Phi is to be taught to talk cleverly by Unjust Cause.

SECOND PARABASIS (lines 1113 - 1130)

The Chorus speaks to the Judges about the comedy contest and urges them to vote for this play.

EPISODE (lines 1131 - 1320)

Several days go by, maybe weeks. Strep, like a good father, stops by the school to find out how Phi is doing. He learns from Socrates that the boy is an excellent student. Happy as can be, Strep greets his son. Phi gives an exhibition of his newly acquired skills. A money-lender comes asking for, what else, money. Strep refuses to pay him because the man makes an error in gender. A second money-lender is turned away similarly by Strep using his new skills.(Perhaps using the wrong article this time?)
In the middle of a meal sometime later, Strep runs out of the house because his boy beats up on him.

SECOND AGON (lines 1321 - 1452)

Strep and Phi argue over the beating. Phi says he beat up his father because his father used to beat up on him when he was a kid. Strep admits he has lost and Phi goes in the house to prove that it is also just to beat up one's mother.

EXODOS (lines 1453 - 1510)

All this proves just a little too much for poor old Strep and he admits that he has actually ruined the boy by leading him down the wrong path and he regrets his error. He then goes to the Thinkery with his slave and begins to demolish the school driving out Socrates and his disciples. (Maybe we should do the same thing with Madison Avenue).

FROGS

CHARACTERS

Dionysus	God of Wine
Xanthias - KSAN -THEE' - AS	his slave
Charon	the Feryman at the River Styx
Aeacus - EH - AH - CUS	a judge in Hades (Hell)
Heracles	a hero and a strong man
Euripides	you know him
Aeschylus	you know him too
Hades	King of the Underworld
Chorus of Frogs	
Chorus of Initiates in the Mysteries	

PLOT

PROLOGUE (lines 1 - 208)

Dionysus enters disguised as Heracles A.K.A HERCULES . He wears the formal tragic garb but also Heracles' trademarks - the lion skin and the club. Xanthias, his slave, is on a donkey and carries luggage on his shoulder. The two are trying ribald jokes (otherwise known as dirty jokes). Xanthias - Xan - starts complaining about the weight he's been carrying, but Dionysus says that the donkey is carrying Xan and therefore the whole weight. They stop by Heracles' house and knock on the door.

Heracles sees Dionysus and roars with laughter. Dionysus discloses that he is obsessed by the great, but dead, poet Euripides, and he is bound and determined to go to Hades and bring him back because the new writers are not as good or as tricky as Euripides was. He says he's stopped by to ask Heracles directions because he (Heracles that is) had been there in the past (Heracles had gone to Hades to seize Cerberus the three-headed dog that watched the entrance to the Underworld - believe this one if you want). Heracles, in jest, suggests three ways to get there quickly, but unfortunately they all involve ...... suicide. Then Heracles tells him the usual route but he is very graphic in describing the horrors that one meets on the way in order to frighten Dionysos.

Xan is still complaining about the weight as a funeral procession comes by. Dionysus greets the dead man and goes on to ask him to take the weight that Xan has on his shoulders to Hades with him. The dead man, being no dummy, asks for a healthy transportation fee for the job so the weight remains on Xan's shoulders.

Continuing on their way, the two reach the banks of the River Styx and see the old ferryman, Charon, who, imagine the gall, refuses to take Xan because he is a slave and has not had any military service, so poor Xan leaves on foot and Charon demands Dionysus to do the rowing. (I don't know what happened to the donkey but clearly the expression "Who pays the ferryman?" must have been created then.)

FIRST PARODOS (lines 209 - 270)

The Chorus of Frogs keeps cadence for the rowing Dionysos using and repeating the refrain VREKEKEX-COAX-COAX, VREKEKEX-COAX-COAX ad nauseum.

EPISODE (lines 271 - 353)

On the other side of the River Styx, Dionysos pays his fare to Charon and meets Xan. They are both scared by the darkness and the sights of the Underworld. Dionysos, rushes across the Orchestra to his priest sitting in the VIP section of the theatron and asks for protection. (A god asking a priest for protection - ha ha ha.) A flute is playing as they watch (Xan and Dionysos, that is) from a hiding spot.

SECOND PARODOS (lines 354 - 459)

The Chorus of Initiates this time comes in singing hymns to, who else but, Dionysos.

There are many satirical references to contempory Athenian VIPs and the Chorus asks the unitiated to leave. They sing more hymns, this time also to Athena and Demeter, besides Dionysos and they ask them to be guided in their celebration and frolicking. Dionysos comes out of hiding and joins in the wild dance. The Chorus again satirizes more Athenian VIPs but finally gives directions how to enter Hades' palace.

EPISODE (lines 460 - 673)

Dionysos locates Hades' palace and knocks on the door. Aeacus, one of the Underworld's judges, upon seeing Dionysos, takes him for Heracles the way he was dressed and calls the guards to arrest him for theft. (Remember Cerberus?) Dionysos is scared stiff (that's something for a god) and offers Xan to change costumes with him, not only that, but he's also willing to carry the luggage (still no word about a donkey).

Once the exchange is settled, one of Persephone's maids comes, greets and welcomes Xan, thinking he is Heracles, and invites him to a feast and fun and more frolicking.

Dionysos, this times says that he was fooling before, and makes Xan switch costumes with him again. He was no fool and Persephone's maid was cute besides. No sooner is the switch accomplished than the landlady of an inn appears and accuses Dionysos, dressed as Heracles, for failing to pay a huge bill at the inn the last time he was in Hades and threatens to call her attorney. Once again Dionysos and Xan change costumes. Aeacus and the guards arrive. Poor Xan is overpowered easily, but he's not stupid either, so he offers his slave Dionysos for questioning by torture. At this point, Dionysos has had it. He has switched clothing several times and has almost always worn the wrong costume. So he gives up and reveals who he really is. Well, there certainly is a doubt as to who the god and who the slave is, so they decide to find out by whipping them. Both of them however cry out in pain, so Aeacus, at a loss, decides to take them both in front of King Hades for identification. Dionysos says at this point that it would have been great had they thought of that before the whipping.

PARABASIS (lines 674 - 737)

The Chorus, addressing the audience, abuses the politician Cleophon, but praises the citizens of Athens. They urge an amnesty for some reactionaries of a few years past who are exiled or have lost their citizenship. Then they satirize another politician Cligenes and urge the Athenians to honor older citizen families more than newer ones.

EPISODE (lines 738 - 894)

Aeacus now knows who the real Dionysus is. He and Xan have become good friends. Some quarrelling voices are heard and Aeacus explains that it is Aschylus and Euripides arguing over the privilege of eating free at Hades' table. Aeschylus had been there quite some time but since Euripides just came, most think that Euripides should sit in the place of honor. To put an end to the argument, Hades announces a contest, the winner of which will get to sit at his table. The contest is simple. With Dionysus as a judge, seeing that the god happened to come by, the words from the works of the two will be weighed and of course the heaviest will win.The Chorus sings in great anticipation of the event as Dionysus, Aeschylus and Euripides enter. The contestants warm up with a few trial attacks on each other, the Chorus prays to the Muses. Before the beginning of the verbal duel, Euripides prays to Ether and Aeschylus to Demeter.

AGON (lines 895 - 1098)

Aeschylus is being attacked by Euripides because he (Aeschylus) used silent, obscene characters, pompous language with long words and very long choral odes. Not only that but he also dwelled too much on war as a theme and did not brush his teeth before going to bed.

Aeschylus attacks Euripides for too much realism in his language and his characters and for depicting immoral love affairs all the time. Not only that but he also used sophistry and didn't have any patriotic themes, no themes of military courage and too much stress on human weaknesses not strengths. His faith in the gods is also questioned not to mention his belief in indoor plumbing.

EPISODE (lines 1099 - 1499)

Euripides continues his attack on Aeschylus' prologues, tendency to repeat things and themes and very poor choral music.

Aeschylus then criticizes Euripides for being monotonous, for historical inaccuracies, for his choral music which was way out and for mixing up the spoken language with bombastic oratorical language.

Right then the scale is brought out and each of the contestants recites a verse from one of their plays into it with the appropriate pomp.

Three repeated times Aeschylus wins because the meanings of his words are on weighty subjects such as rock and iron and incest. Hades enters and learns who has won. Despite the contest, Dionysus still has a hard time deciding. So he dreams up an additional challenge for the contestants. He will give the victory to the one who can give the best practical advice to save the city. Euripides is vague and Aeschylus more vigorous. Dionysus is on the verge of making a final decision when Euripides reminds him that after all it was he who Dionysus had come after not Aeschylus. Despite the reminder, Dionysus chooses Aeschylus quoting Euripides a famous line from Hippolytus. Hades then invites Aeschylus and Dionysus to a farewell dinner and maybe some frolicking.

EXODOS (lines 1500 - 1533)

Right after dinner, Hades sends Aeschylus off to Athens, urging him to aid the city anyway he can. One way would be with death dealing gifts for known persons in Athens which Hades gives to him and tells Aeschylus to tell these people that Hades is anxious to see them and soon.

Aeschylus, who can hold a grudge, asks that Sophocles be put at the honor table instead of him and that they exclude Euripides forever. What a sore winner, kicking the loser when he's down! The Chorus bid him a fond farewell.

Enrol is the same as enroll. If in doubt, look it up.

DionysOs and DionysUs is one and the same god. For the sake of variety if not confusion, both are used interchangably!

SOME NOTES ON ARISTOPHANES WHICH I TOOK WHILE BORED IN SOME UNIVERSITY IN THE UPPER MID-WEST REGION OF THE USA

Aristophanes is, or rather was, because he's long gone, the first literary critic in history. I'm not so sure he did us any favors for paving the way. In the Clouds he satirizes Euripides vigorously and we also see some criticism of Aeschylus but he finally saves him in the end.

Aristophanes was a conservative with traditional ideas and he opposed any new ideas that came along, so he was critical of intellectuals like the Sophists. He also criticized the weaknesses in democracy, new radical economic theories and in general anything new was radical to him.

Exaggeration and caricature was his means of satire. He was witty with sharp comic imagination for situations. His poetry was remarkable as well as his ribald jests and vulgar farce which to me would be a difficult thing to combine. Almost like putting Tennyson and Xaviera Hollander in the same line.

IV
EPILOGUE

(and other fun things)

EPILOGUE
not really but...

Now you all know who Oedipus really was, don't you? One thing I neglected to mention through all the bewailing and bemoaning was that the name Oedipus means ......"Swollen Foot". Well, I really did not forget. It just seemed the wrong thing to say while reading tragedy, not that other wrong things were not mentioned, but a Big Foot relative seemed, at the time, a little too much. In retrospect maybe not. It certainly was not a nice name to give to a child. No wonder he killed his dad. Can you imagine the teasing in school?

Through this brief and sometimes tediously monotonous, or should I say monotonously tedious, summary and pseudo-analysis, I hope you were introduced or re-introduced to classical drama in a non-classical way. Certainly, one can see why and how classical drama has been a model imitated in unclassical ways by today's theater, movies and television. For thousands of years, as long as there are people, the people's problems remain the same hence the themes repeat themselves. The old Greeks were the first ones to dramatize them.

As for me, an imitation Greek, I am still looking for my Deus-ex-machina. Quietly.

SOME COMMONLY ASKED QUESTIONS
AND
SOME UNCOMMONLY GIVEN ANSWERS

QUESTION- Why did they (have to) use such ghastly names? Why didn't they use names like say Bob, Joe, Marty, Alice,Pat, Tom, Dick or even Harry & Charlie?
ANSWER - Your guess is as good as mine. It could have been because of acute subliminal depression and a slightly obtuse cynical sense.

QUES.-Why did they use masks to begin with?
ANS.- They thought it was cute!

Q.- Was Oedipus for real?
A.- Indeed he was! Much to his credit however, he really felt badly about it once he found out.

Q.- Did his mother accuse him of sexual harassment?
A.- A definitive NO.

Q.- Is there a difference between comedy and tragedy?
A.- Why, should there be any?

Q. - Did the ancient actors overact with the same pomposity and gusto as modern Greek actors do?

A.- Nobody really knows with any certainty the answer to this frequently asked question. However my totally unbiased guess is that that would be not just plainly unlikely, but impossible. Nobody, but nobody can possibly outdo the modern "actors".

Q.- Why did they wear those silly costumes?
A.- Christianos Dioropoulos, the pre-eminent costume designer of the 5th cetury B.C., had a refreshingly wonderful sense of the absurd.

Q.- Did the Chorus always drag their feet or did they actually dance sometimes?
A.- Choreography as we know it and love it today, had not been created yet. It was not until 1938 A.D. that it was introduced in Las Vegas, Nevada and the Radio City Music Hall in New York, simultaneously.

Q.- I can see a title like The House of Atreus or even Oedipus Rex, but ...... FROGS ?
A.- It must have been a momentary lapse in Aristophanes' usually keen mind, because his other plays had much more commercially acceptable titles such as Birds, Wasps, e.t.c. Or maybe he was putting the Athenians on.

Q.- Is VREKEKEX-COAX-COAX a real word and if so what is its etymology?

A.- Indeed it is a very real word which in fact, had remained intact throughout the ages , and up to 1971, sometime in April, when the youth of Greece suddenly fell into an educational coma and the word became extinct. Etymologically, thorough research indicates that it was coined in the 6th century B.C., by a deaf Athenian who thought that this must be the sound that female frogs make while mating. The last part came into the English language with the invention of the coaxial speaker systems in the 1950s.

BIBLIOGRAPHY?

AESCHYLUS
Prometheus bound
Agamemnon
Choephoroe
Eumenides

EURIPIDES
Trojan Women
Medea
Hippolytus
Electra

SOPHOCLES
Oedipus Rex
Oedipus at Colonus
Antigone
Electra

ARISTOPHANES
Birds
Clouds
Frogs

But also:Needleman, Sandor. *Time, Essence, and Reality. A Systematic Reevaluation of Nothingness.*(New York, 1975)

Non-Existence. What to do if it Suddenly strikes you. (New York, 1975)

Semantic Modes of Non-Essential Functioning. (New York,?)

Remedial Latin (Athens 1907)

THE MORALS OF THE PLAYS AT A GLANCE

Doing abominations is against the moral law, but if you must, do them in moderation. (also Woody Allen)

Whosoever shall not fall by the sword or by famine, shall fall by pestilence, so why bother shaving? (Woody Allen)

Roses are red, violets are blue
I'm schizophrenic, and so am I. (Key West T-shirt)
Do unto others as you'd have others do unto you, but do it first. (anon)

Whosoever killeth their father, or mother or children there'll be hell to pay.

It's best to keep one's very own prurient interests to oneself and under control at all times.

Holy smokes, who'll pay the ferryman?
Hell hath no fury like a woman scorned. (See where William S. got this one from?)

Never try to pacify someone at the height of his rage.

Everybody is somebody else's weirdo. (A. Bloch)

Anyone who is popular is bound to be disliked. (Y. Berra)

Say no, then negotiate. (Helga)
He who is perverse in his ways will fall into a pit. (Proverbs 28,18)

A good name is better than a precious ointment. (Ecclesiastes 7,1)

Dead flies make the perfumers ointment give off an evil odor. (Ecclesiastes 10,1)

Cursed be he who lies with his father's wife. (Deuteronomy 27,20)

(Since we are on a biblical kick, you'll forgive a momentary digression, which however, will solve something that may have been bothering you for years without knowing it.

"Then Cain went away from the presence of the LORD, and dwelt in the land of Nod, east of Eden." Genesis 4,16
Now you know where the title for the James Dean movie came from. Not only that, but had you not read or seen "Inherit the Wind" with Spencer Tracy you could not have known who Cain had married. See, there was another land besides Eden. A question that has forever been bothering theologians has been who had created the land of Nod without them knowing it.)

All of the above was not a thoughtless, mindless digression. It had a purpose which was to show you why human beings are what they are and need Morality Plays to make them Moral. You see that we are only partially descended from the Garden of Eden. Our other half came from the land of Nod which was away from the presence of the Lord. Now doesn't this explain a whole lot?

WHAT OTHERS SAY

Poor Natasha! All the typing she had to do.

Mandy Mukas

Who is this Natasha anyway and what does she see in him?

His ex-wives

No, not again dad!

His three sons in unison

I didn't know Greek drama was so.........dramatic.

Chris Moukas

Vernon seems capable of being unfunny.

Literary critic-deceased

Vile, nasty and licentious but will it sell?

Anon. enemy

Well, I don't think it's all that bad. Nevertheless I'm glad I didn't have to buy it. He gave me one you know, for Christmas.

His mother

BY THE SAME AUTHOR

1 & 2 GREEK-A FRACTURED LEXICON
Two volumes of absolutely and hysterically funnyidioms and phrases.

3 A VISITORS GUIDE TO MODERN GREEK BEHAVIOR & HABITS
A tongue-in-cheek approach to the culture shock.

4 A VISITORS GUIDE TO GREEK DRIVING? AND OTHER OXYMORA & PARADOXA
1001 things a visitor needs to know in order to survive or just to laugh.

5 GREECE WITHOUT TEARS
Suggestions for the non-touristy tourist.

6 A VISITORS GUIDE TO GREEK DRAMA unclassical approach to some classics.

ABOUT THE AUTHOR

Mr.Elliott is his mother's only human child, an eccentric one at that. (eccentric being a flattering if not euphemistic description). Having decided that it is never too late to have a happy child-hood, he opted to have one instead of a mid-life crisis, in mid- life of course. He loves to fly his kites at Sounion or anywhere for that matter, can't sit stillwhen he hears either Sambas or Greek Island Dances or any other noble and gentle beat, and sails all over the world looking for them. He has discovered that the best place to hear Greek Island music is paradoxically either America or Australia and conversely he has danced many a samba on Greek islands! His sailboat "Kariba" in Swahili -a very succint language- is the Salvador Dali dictum "The only difference between a madman and me is that I am Not Mad." Coincidentally in Urdu it means "Why be Normal?"

Mr. Elliott does not fancy himself as a writer-nobody else does as a matter of fact -and is not looking forward to growing up lest he has to make up his mind what he is going to become or what is to become of him- Whichever comes first.

don't miss

vernon's

new hot off the press sensation

SEX

as

a

SECOND LANGUAGE

Gregory of Nyssa. (49)

t 54 . Morwenna Ludlow OUP. 2007.

Prosopon commonly meant a theatrical role, and this could give the impression of one undifferentiated God playing different roles at different stages of salvation history

[illegible]